THE FORTRESS

Echoes of War

THE FORTRESS
A Diary of
Anzio and After

RALEIGH TREVELYAN

BUCHAN & ENRIGHT, PUBLISHERS
LONDON

First published in 1956 by William Collins Sons & Co. Ltd
Re-published in 1972 by Leo Cooper Ltd

This edition published in 1985 by
Buchan & Enright, Publishers, Limited
53 Fleet Street, London EC4Y 1BE

British Library Cataloguing in Publication Data

Trevelyan, Raleigh
    The Fortress
    1. Great Britain, Army, Green Howards   2. Anzio
    Beachhead, 1944   3. World War, 1939–1945
    —Personal narratives, British
    I. Title
    940.54'81'0941   D763.182A6
    ISBN 0-907675-52-2

Printed in Great Britain by
Redwood Burn Limited, Trowbridge, Wiltshire and
bound by Pegasus Bookbinding, Melksham, Wiltshire
Cover printed by The Furnival Press, London

FOR MY MOTHER
AND IN MEMORY OF T.P.L.,
G.L.S. AND C.W.N.

CONTENTS

RETURN TO ANZIO

INTRODUCTION

WHEN *The Fortress* was first published, I left out the name of my regiment. It was the Rifle Brigade. At Anzio I was attached to the Green Howards in the 5th or Y (Yorkshire) Division, and we relieved the 56th or Black Cat Division. Later, at the beginning of July, I rejoined the Rifle Brigade.

I also changed the names of my three friends who were killed. 'Monty' was Charles Newton, 'Kip' was Jimmy Stevens, and 'Toumi' was Timmy Lloyd. Of course one was not really allowed to keep a diary in the line, but for me then it was a compulsion. I did my best to leave out things that would be of military significance. However the whole Anzio experience weighed on me so much that a year later I rewrote the diary, putting in everything I could remember. When I was preparing the book for publication I also used some letters that my mother had kept. It was Timmy Lloyd's death that eventually decided me to give up keeping a diary altogether.

At the end of November, 1944, I got a job in the Military Mission in Rome, where I mostly was for two years. In that way I came to know and love Central Italy as much as anywhere in the world. Yet I always avoided going back to Anzio. Finally in 1968 I did return, and I wrote what I felt for the *Observer*, which published my article in January the following year, on the 25th anniversary of the Anzio landings. The article is printed at the end of this book, with some passages omitted as they were more or less lifted from *The Fortress*. My return was an exorcism. I was freed of Anzio for ever.

RALEIGH TREVELYAN

PART ONE

Anzio

THE first landings at Anzio were on 22nd January, 1944. I was in Algiers at the time.

During February the Germans made a great effort to oust the Allies from the Beachhead. Losses on both sides were heavy, and the British and Americans were forced back to limits where there could be no further retreat. However, by 1st March it was obvious that the Germans had accepted the fact that they had failed, and their drive began rapidly to peter out.

On my arrival in Italy I had to join the battalion of another regiment, not my own. We were sent as reinforcements to Anzio on 2nd March, and within twenty-four hours were at a place nicknamed *The Fortress*, one of the key defensive positions in the Beachhead and the nearest to Rome. I was a subaltern, aged twenty, and had never before been in action.

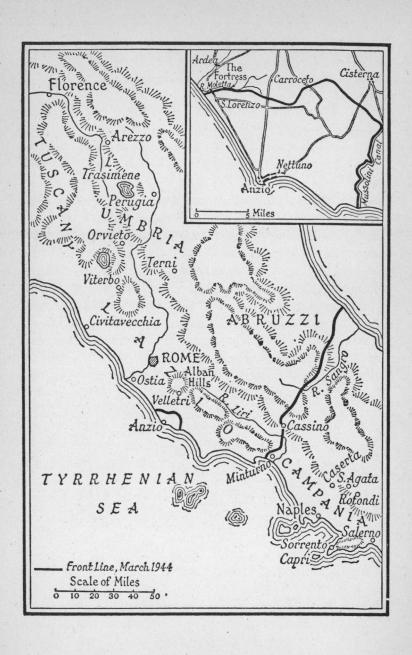

Florence

TUSCANY

Arezzo

L. Trasimène

Perugia

UMBRIA

Orvieto

Terni

Viterbo

L. Civitavecchia

ABRUZZI

ROME

Ostia Alban Hills

Velletri R. Liri

Anzio

Cassino

Minturno

R. Sangro

Caserta

S. Agata

Rofondi

CAMPANIA

Naples

Sorrento

Capri

Salerno

TYRRHENIAN SEA

Ardea

The Fortress

R. Moletta

S. Lorenzo

Carroceto

Cisterna

Nettuno

Anzio

Mussolini Canal

5 Miles

Front Line, March 1944

Scale of Miles

0 10 20 30 40 50

THE FORTRESS

Two nights ago we returned from the Fortress. I am writing this in my sand-hole at B Echelon (how to translate B Echelon into ordinary language I don't know, but it means out of the line anyway). The sea is only a few hundred yards off, separated from us by high dunes massed over with tamarisks and umbrella pines. In the distance, towards the Alban Hills, we hear the desultory firing of heavy artillery, and sometimes a stray round goes rustling overhead. I have done practically nothing else but sleep since I came back. . . .

Our officers' mess is in the back of a three-tonner. Major Babworth and the rest sit there all day long, and most of the night, on overturned ration boxes playing cribbage and drinking rye whisky. Those damned fools have one-track minds; they aren't able to get away from shop. 'God, the Fortress was a picnic compared to the cemetery at Minturno,' etc., etc. Then they start off on How We Crossed the Catania Plain. As if I were interested. Yet I must write down what happened at the Fortress. . . .

Sergeant Chesterton had gone ahead earlier that evening and was ready to greet us when we arrived at our platoon area. I barely had the chance of exchanging more than a few words with the officer from whom I was taking over; he was obviously on edge and even in the starlight I could see huge pouches of weariness under his eyes. For my part, I was not yet accustomed to the racket of gunfire and of shells whizzing backwards and forwards, whilst my back and shoulders were still aching after the long march up. All the officer did in fact say to me was: 'Oh, hallo. Good show. You've arrived.' And then, when I started to question him about the direction of the enemy, Sergeant Chesterton at once cut in and said that he (Sergeant Chesterton) knew all the details and I was not to worry. With that, the officer forced a vague smile at me and hurried off to catch up the rest of his platoon, who were already slithering down the muddy slope into the valley.

It turned out that the enemy was about seventy yards away. Until daylight came, I was not able to get a clear impression of the country around us. Bushes seemed to block the view everywhere, although the sergeant said that we had a clear field of fire of at least thirty yards. My trench, which I shared with Viner, my batman, was plumb in the centre of the platoon area, so close to the other trenches that I could call to each of my section commanders in a loud whisper.

We were to find ourselves on the edge of a small thickly wooded valley. (Most of the Beachhead apparently consists of flat grassland, through which these deep tangly valleys, or wadis as the men call them, run like fissures from some primeval earthquake.) Company Headquarters was behind us, down below; we had passed by it before reaching the platoon area – a sort of mud kraal, bolstered up with sandbags and surrounded by the white crosses of temporary graves.

One advantage of being so close to the Germans was that we were within the minimum range of their mortars. Snipers and hand grenades were the main worry, not counting shells falling short and airbursts. All night long

16

the artillery and mortars of both sides kept up a non-stop barrage. The screeching and whirring of the shells over our héads might have been some furious gathering of witches on Walpurgis Night. Sometimes the explosions were close enough for us to see shreds of flames spurting upwards in the dark, and the shrapnel would come hissing at us on all sides. We grew to distinguish the sound of various guns, as if they were voices – some were alto, some bass, some grumbly, some like baying wolves, some as retchy as the cough of a tubercular in his last stages. But all these were more or less noises off; nearer to hand were the staccato *eugh-eugh* of two-inch mortars, the snarly spandau-ripple, the more deliberate bren-crackle, and the swift searing whine past of a single bullet, generally tracer and half-seen like a miniature comet. Often a corner of the sky would be illuminated with gaudy showers of multi-hued Very lights. ... Although a small battle started up on the opposite side of the wadi, and several grenades went off, we had a quietish time the first night at the Fortress and were hardly troubled at all by the Germans.

It had been raining a good deal for some days before our arrival, and this at first seemed to account for the heavy cloying smell everywhere, like fungus. I soon discovered that the smell mostly came from empty bully and 'conner' (or stew, Maconochie's) tins chucked unburied into the bushes. In addition, the previous platoon had been none too particular about the disposal of human excreta. ...

There were about two inches of *café au lait* coloured water at the bottom of our trench, and so Viner and I had to sit hunched up on ration boxes, occasionally easing our joints by sticking out our feet on to each other's knees. Blankets had been used to line the trench, in order to stop the earth from falling in, but these had become so soggy that we had to avoid leaning against them. It was impossible to find a dry place where we could stand our tommy cookers for brewing up or heating the conner, so we had to construct a special platform of empty bren mags supported on broken bayonets.

Not long after dawn that first morning a man called Baxter, a sort of puffy-faced charwoman in battledress, came crawling over, eyes popping out. A dead Jerry, covered with a ground sheet, was in the next trench to his, he said, and neither his mate nor he could stand the thought of it. Sergeant Chesterton scoffed at him, and said that he might like to know that there were seven more dead Tedeschi (i.e. Jerries) strewn around the platoon area. Apparently two weeks previously these Jerries – in the sergeant's words – had come striding through the bushes, looking this way and that, wondering where the bloody hell to throw their grenades. 'But our brens were waiting and gave them the old what for. Now their pals won't be coming this way again in a hurry.'

I then realized the significance of certain bundles of blue-grey rags in the undergrowth ahead of us. Sergeant Chesterton ordered another fellow, a kosher butcher in civilian life ('He's used to dealing with dead meat'), to shovel some earth over Baxter's Jerry. The last platoon, I was told, had been too bomb-happy to attempt to bury the corpses. Not that there had been any scruples about stripping them of watches and valuables; Sergeant Chesterton had already been out 'to have a dekko' and had found the ground littered with papers and the contents of the Jerries' wallets. It was with relish that he told me of the achievements of Pezner, the kosher butcher, who was reputed to have sucked rings from dead men's fingers. 'We'll have to nab a nice rich Tedesch for *you*,' he said, sizing up the watch that I had won once in a church fête raffle at home.

I came across another of these corpses when scouting about for a suitable place to dig a latrine. He had been an N.C.O. Looking at the drained waxy features of my first dead body, I felt only curiosity. His eyes were open and his teeth were like spillikins, too far apart. Lots of photographs, flabby from the rain, were lying in the mud beside him. I chose one to show to Sergeant Chesterton; it was of a group of men, smiling spillikin smiles and with naked torsos, perched in comradely attitudes on the back of a truck, probably in the Desert.

Every time I so much as glanced out of my dugout, my eyes were drawn involuntarily to the blue-grey bundles. The fungus-smell took on a new significance, and Baxter kept beefing about the corpse in his adjoining trench; so I decided to approach Major Babworth when I was on my next routine visit to Company H.Q. I suggested to him that we might carry the Jerries down on a stretcher, for burial somewhere. Major Babworth was merely irritated. 'What, pick 'em up when they're over two weeks gone? They'll crumble to bits at a touch. Far more useful to rig 'em up as scarecrows – scare-Jerries, rather.' And the pun so pleased him that he repeated it several times over. . . .

After light the artillery fire, and most enemy activity, would die down almost entirely. Day was therefore turned into night for the purpose of sleeping and we would take it in turns to have two hours' rest whilst the other member of the trench was on stag, or on guard. As soon as dusk came, all the excitements – patrols, etc. – started up, so everyone had to keep on the alert from then until dawn. Viner was a terrible snorer, and we had constantly to wake him up in case he gave our position away. He came from Bristol and had a somewhat negroid appearance, with crimped black hair, thick lips and an oily skin; other members of the platoon said that he was never known to have smiled, let alone crack a joke. At first I allowed him to do all the cooking, such as it was, but his hands were so caked with dirt that I had to take it over myself.

I had a copy of Keats in my pack, and the first volume of the Oxford *War and Peace*. Everyone had said that 'doing nothing' was the worst part of trench warfare. I managed Book I of *War and Peace* – Anna Palovna's drawing-room and all that – but descriptions of Cossacks retreating along the Danube hardly make escapist reading. . . .

Because of the noise that the water-tins made when they clanked together, we avoided fetching the rations at night. However, the route we had to take was exposed to snipers, and a couple of my men got nasty wounds and had to be sent back to B Echelon. We often heard the sound of Jerries digging, generally just after dawn. Sometimes we heard them talking too; each time they seemed closer to us than on the previous occasion. It was hard to whip up any interest about these things at H.Q.; Major Babworth scarcely stirred from his kraal, and just lounged on his bunk smoking Bruno's and using foul language. Every time I went in there, he would lecture me on how the whole Beachhead would be lost if the Fortress were overrun.

One morning we glimpsed the square shape of a Jerry Panzer helmet moving across the gap in front of us. Sergeant Chesterton and Bishop, who shared his trench, insisted on putting wire across the same gap later in the day. We had every bren covering them, in case they ran into trouble and the German trenches were nearer than we expected. I was also afraid that the gap might have been mined – just the sort of thing that the bomb-happies in the previous platoon would have forgotten to tell us about. But all went smoothly, although afterwards it certainly did seem as if we had roused the Jerries' suspicions. In the afternoon we were very bothered by odd bullets whipping over, presumably from a sniper. One tore a ragged hole in the ground sheet on the edge of the trench above my head. Then, during the same night, an enemy patrol was sent out. We distinctly heard the Jerries making bird noises at each other as they crept about in the bushes – a favourite trick of theirs, so Sergeant Chesterton said. But we withheld our fire, as we had been ordered by Company H.Q. not to give away the exact dispositions of our trenches unless absolutely vital.

Luckily we didn't have to do any patrolling ourselves. This was done for us by a group of Commandos, who were attached to Company H.Q. They were wiry little fellows, always wearing cap comforters and with faces muddied for camouflage. Nothing seemed to give them more pleasure than unnecessary discomfort. . . .

The wadi branched into two, just where we were. We could see a ruined house above the offshoot that went into enemy territory. On several occasions we watched Jerries nonchalantly walking about there, brewing up or even relieving themselves. I managed to get the company sergeant-major to come up and look at them, but he said that they were too far away for sniping at and too near for the mortars, and, anyway, there was this keep-mum policy at the moment. Neither we nor the Germans, evidently, were at all sure of the layout of each other's positions. There was no properly defined *line* between us. One night a couple of Jerries stumbled by mistake into our Company H.Q.; they were carrying a dixie of soup (greasy muck with lumps of black bread in it, so the C.S.M. said). It seemed that they weren't proper soldiers at all, but civilians, farm labourers from Eastern Europe, who were being used as cooks and general dogsbodies. They gave H.Q. a lot of useful information.

Our second night at the Fortress I noticed figures

moving on the ridge above the opposite side of the wadi,
where our neighbouring company had another platoon. I
rang up on the field telephone to warn Major Babworth,
and soon afterwards the other platoon opened up with its
brens. When morning came, a coil of Jerry wire was
plainly visible on the ridge, with a blue-grey corpse
sprawled alongside. We couldn't spot any movement the
following night, but by morning there was more wire to
be seen, and the corpse had disappeared. The morning
after that there was more wire still.

Then I was told that it was my turn to move to the
forward platoon area, the one that was the closest to
Rome in the entire Beachhead. The move had to be done
at night, and first of all we had to go into an intermediate
position. Perhaps it's easier if I draw a map.

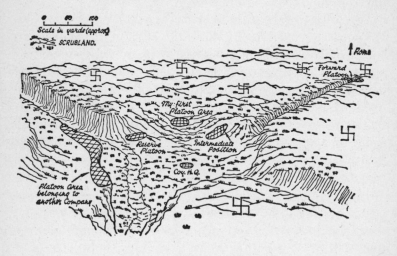

You will see that to get to the forward position we had
to go along a small valley, running through no-man's-
land.

Mike Harper's platoon was in this intermediate position and we had to change places, so that there would be

22

as little distance as possible for me to travel when I went on to the forward area. My platoon would remain in the intermediate position for twenty-four hours. That very evening of our changeover, Mike – always a little crackpot at the best of times – developed a sudden mania for firing his two-inch mortar, much to the disapproval, I heard later, of Major Babworth. His targets were presumed to be the Jerry trenches somewhere ahead of my platoon, and often his bombs dropped uncomfortably close. I rang him up three times and begged him to lay off, but he took no notice. Finally a bomb dropped short in his own platoon area; in fact, it exploded just as it left the barrel. There were several bad casualties, and Mike himself was considerably shaken. All this resulted in my having to plan out every detail of the changeover between the two platoons. . . .

I said that zero hour would be eleven o'clock. At nearly half past ten, just as I was beginning to gather my kit together, a man dragged himself over to me. He seemed apologetic. 'Excuse me,' he said, 'Corporal says he can hear Jerries advancing through them bushes.'

I beckoned him to slip into the trench beside me.

The wind was rustling the dead leaves. We strained for some sign of movement. Then a bird called, a curious hoarse note. Another answered, more shrilly. But were they from an enemy patrol? We still couldn't be sure.

Half an hour passed. It was zero hour. The first section under Corporal Peter hoisted on their packs with maddening clumsiness. Bren magazines were kicked about; tommy butts slapped against tree trunks and branches.

At last I joined Corporal Peter and together we led the way to the wire, the same wire that Sergeant Chesterton and Bishop had put up two days earlier. In the darkness ahead there was a scuffle, and rattle of bolts.

'Quick, ambush!'

23

Corporal Peter snatched a bren from the man behind him, and we both leapt into a trench, miraculously to hand.

'You take the right shadow. I'll take the left.'

We fired blindly, orange flames bursting from my tommy. Corporal Peter flung a grenade. Then something flew overhead and plopped behind us. A Jerry grenade. More firing. Then silence.

(Next morning I had to send up a runner, a member of Corporal Peter's section, to collect some ammunition from Mike Harper. The runner told me that he'd seen a dead Jerry in the bush at which I'd been firing. My first kill!)

Eventually we decided to get going again. A new moon had risen, giving us less chance of concealment if we met another ambush. The way down was very slippery. I kept remembering the silver St. Christopher's medal my mother had given me the last time I saw her in England. Over and over I repeated the words inscribed on it: '*St. Christophe te protège. St. Christophe te protège.*'

Mike was very rude about the delays. He started haranguing me, and was only stopped by a heavy downpour of rain, which continued for some hours and soaked our clothes right through. . . .

There was a wonderfully vulgar sunrise. Everything was the colour of pink geraniums, and birds were singing. We felt as Noah must have done when he saw his rainbow. Suddenly Viner pointed across the stretch of scrubby heath. An individual, dressed in German uniform, was wandering like a sleep-walker across our line of fire. It was clear that for the moment he had forgotten war, and – as we had been doing – was revelling in the promise of warmth and spring.

'Shall I bump him off?' asked Viner, without a note of expression in his voice.

24

I had to decide quickly. 'No,' I replied, 'just scare him away.'

Viner aimed above the man's head, and fired. The Jerry turned for a moment or two, stared at us with mouth open, then went bounding through the trees, waving his rifle above his head.

'Another bomb-happy,' said Bishop, who happened to be standing by us, and he gave him a parting shot.

Only Sergeant Chesterton didn't laugh. He said that we should have killed the fellow, since his friends would now be told precisely where our trenches were.

We were able to move about much more freely this time, and so we took the opportunity of cleaning and oiling our weapons, changing our underclothes, and putting on dry socks. My feet were crinkled and yellow-white, like a hen's after boiling. I insisted that everybody should have a shave and brush his teeth. (It's surprising how physical appearances affect morale.) We had great difficulty coping with a tough nut called Crocker, a real old soldier. He hadn't shaved once since we'd left B Echelon, and would only do so when Sergeant Chesterton threatened to put him on permanent latrine duty the moment we returned out of the line.

Again at 11 p.m. that night we made our way to the new area, the forward position. To get there we had to push through straggling branches and creepers along a narrow stream-bed, with steep wet banks on each side. It was Adrian's platoon that we were having to relieve. I was glad to see dear old Adrian's features again. Before he left, he told me some garbled tale about how he had crawled over a ridge and come face to face with a German officer eating spaghetti in a dugout. At night, he said, the enemy mounted a machine-gun-cum-observation post at the head of the wadi. And sure enough, if you raised yourself high enough under the left-hand bank, you could see the machine-gun silhouetted against the sky.

It rained all the time we were in that position. Our feet were soaked and we had no blankets. Company H.Q. used to send up a sackful of fresh socks each night. We could hardly stir because the Germans were so close, and the only way to keep warm was to wriggle about inside your clothes, so creating a friction against the coarse 'issue' army vest. A single strand of telephone wire connected us to H.Q.; it wasn't really much use as a means of communication, as we could only speak very very softly, with our voices muffled.

During the day we could hear our opposite numbers over the ridge prattling away to one another, laughing and even singing. We came to recognize the voices of at least two of them, one called Leo and another with a name like Moupi. It was a pity nobody in our platoon could understand what they were saying (all those years wasted playing the fool in German classes at school). Sometimes we smelt cooking and heard tins knocking together as the Jerries evidently queued up for their meals. We, on the other hand, couldn't so much as brew up a mugful of tea.

The men looked purple from the cold, and it needed will-power to stop your teeth from chattering. A special allocation of rum used to come up from H.Q. with the socks, and before dawn I crawled round every trench with a spoon and the flask.

The second night a grenade exploded, up on the bank where I had one of my sections. Someone was badly hurt, as we heard him crying out for a long while. We had no idea whether it was one of our men or not, until Sergeant Chesterton climbed up there and reported back that the grenade had been thrown by Bishop at a Jerry, reputedly only fifteen yards away. Next morning I myself went to look for the body, but it had disappeared, although the blood on the grass still looked new.

That grenade of Bishop's must have started to alarm the Jerries, for on the third night – our last before we were due to be relieved – we were attacked by a fighting patrol, and a shower of grenades came over. We beat the Jerries off, and nobody was hurt – on either side, it seemed. Then, whilst the rain pelted down, the machine-gun loosed off tracer down the wadi. We in Platoon H.Q. had to flatten ourselves against the banks, whilst the bullets streaked past only a couple of feet off. I had Crocker with me, and quite suddenly he broke down and started to cry, saying, 'Oh, oh,' so loudly that I had to put my hand over his mouth in case the Jerries heard.

We were expecting runners with the rations, etc., just at the same time as the machine-gun was firing. The telephone was on the other side of the wadi and so I couldn't reach it to ring up and warn H.Q. However, the row must have kept the runners back, for they didn't turn up until nearly light. They were in such a hurry to get away again, whispering and stumbling over water-tins, that the machine-gun treated us to a few more bursts.

Dawn was breaking as the runners left. I had to let Crocker go back with them.

There was complete silence all day from the German lines. That meant they had fairly got the wind up. We were positive that they would launch a proper attack after dark. The question was – would it happen whilst the changeover took place?

A few grenades came over at dusk. I had hardly slept the whole time that I had been in the forward position, and I think that was why I became sick and shivery. I didn't feel inclined to talk much to the relieving officer, a Jock. He had obviously had no conception of the sort of place he was coming to. After I had shown him the ma-

27

chine-gun post he looked so indignant that I was afraid that he would withdraw his platoon and leave us up there in the lurch.

Later, reports came through that the Jerries *did* put in that attack, in the small hours. The Jock lost one man and a number of others were wounded, and so the new company decided to pull out of the position altogether.

And so, now I am back at B Echelon. In two days' time we are off to another part of the front. Today I went to the mobile showers for my first clean-up since I arrived at Anzio. We all lined up together, stark naked, to take our turn under the dribbles of hot water. Suddenly somebody gave me a great slap on the behind, and a voice said: 'Well, if it isn't Mr. Trevelyan.' And there was a Lance-Corporal Smith, whom I hadn't seen since training days at Retford. He was full of the latest news about everyone and how he had been downgraded, because of impacted wisdom teeth, and put into a field bakery. 'And what have you been up to all this while?' he said jovially. . . .

STEAMBOAT BILL'S

24th March

Two hours to go, then twilight and the hush of waiting. We only arrived here yesterday. Lord knows what rules of the game the Germans mean to impose on us. If one of my outposts is attacked, overrun even, how can I possibly send help? The front I am supposed to control is so ridiculously large; it boils down to a series of machine-gun nests, three or four men in each, scattered along hedgerows or in dips like empty dew ponds in the middle of fields. It's too spread out for a company to cope with, let alone a platoon at three-quarter's strength – which is literally my case, now that I have lost so many men in hospital or on leave.

Conditions here are very different from those at the Fortress. For one thing, there are no wadis. For another, the enemy is six or seven hundred yards away. Yet he still has the advantage over us, being concentrated in a dense wood where he can swan around quite freely. The slightest stir on our part brings down a whole heap of mortar fire, and my Platoon H.Q. in this cattle-shed always gets the worst of it – that is, excepting the crossroads behind us, the site of Company H.Q., known as Stonk Corner, stonking meaning shelling in the lingo of this battalion. Company H.Q. is actually located in one of a group of ruined farm buildings, originally painted a dark mustard, looming jaggedly among a few scruffy umbrella pines. But trust Major Babworth to be concreted up in a deep cellar!

Not that we do too badly ourselves. I write this eight foot underground by a shaft of reflected sunshine. American engineers were here before us and have created a real masterpiece, proof against anything except a direct

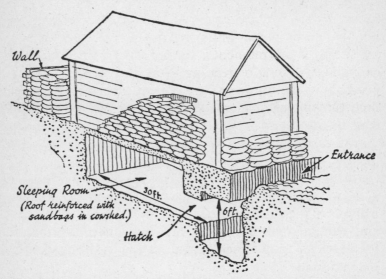

hit. The entrance, at one end of a cowshed – the farthest from the Germans – is protected by sandbags; you lower yourself through a funnel, curtained by a blanket at night, into the main dugout, called the foxhole by the Americans; then, after some complicated gymnastics, you are through a slit, known as the hatch, and on your hands and knees in the straw that covers the floor of the sleeping-room, or dosshouse. This last is *underneath* the cowshed, about thirty foot long, and has a ceiling of thick rafters, earth and more sandbags. In front of the cowshed, and acting as an extra shield against the Germans, is a fair-sized wall, providentially intact although well bashed about farther along.

The Americans maintained that they had been in this same place for forty-one days. Their main trouble, they told us, had been lack of water, and judging by the stink they left behind, I'm not surprised. Washing at present is out of the question – our allowance of water is enough for two mess-tins of tea per head per day. We have no paraffin either, so that means no light in the foxhole at night except by a single fading torch battery. Even during the day there is a Stygian murkiness down here, and where I am sitting at this moment is the only spot with light good enough for writing or reading. Now and then I poke my head above the top for a breather, unexpectedly the first time catching sight of the sea, sparkling like blue tinfoil over the sand-dunes, just half a mile away. And on the other side, to the right, I saw high mountains with snow on them.

The three other members of Platoon H.Q. are asleep, as it is my turn for stag. They are Sergeant Chesterton, Bishop as mortarman, and Squash Williams as runner and wireless operator. With this manpower shortage I found release from Viner and have presented him to one of the bren posts.

Squash is a teetotaller, hence his name. He has a thin rabbity face covered with freckles, tiny pouchy eyes, broad nostrils, and hair like fur. I suppose he must be about thirty, although he looks forty – I've learnt to accept the fact that Anzio makes you look ten years older. The way Squash talks about his 'old woman' and 'me poor legs' you might think he was sixty. Mentally, as he himself puts it, he is a bit off-net, since he can't keep up with our talk (never on high level, even so). Before the war he ran a grocery business outside Leicester, with a pull-in for lorry drivers called Steamboat Bill's as a sideline.

It didn't take him long to discover that the Yanks had bequeathed us a glorious treasury of tinned food, such as

31

we haven't seen for years, even in England. He kept this find a secret from the rest of us until lunchtime; we had wondered why he had been so anxious to be on stag precisely then, involving the unpopular additional duty of having to brew up the compôt tea, mash biscuits into porridge, and slice up bully. When he woke me for lunch, I had been sleeping heavily in the frowstiness of the doss-house, and so for that matter, had Sergeant Chesterton and Bishop. We were not therefore disposed to react to Squash's method of rousing us in the manner that he had doubtless expected. First, he gave each of us a prolonged shaking by the shoulders; next, he rattled a spoon against a mess-tin, while – to the tune of reveillé – he bawled out the words: 'Wakey, wakey, rise and shine. Tiffin-time for lordships mine.' Then he shook us again.

I could hear ominous grunts from the sergeant as, with eyes bunged up and hair full of straw, we hauled our bodies into the foxholes. There we had the spectacle of Squash himself dressed up as a 'chef', with long woollen pants, a very grubby civvy shirt tied round his middle, and a punched-out American sidecap balanced on his head. He had also contrived to give himself a pair of black moustachios and a pointed beard.

He must have scented trouble, for he quickly whipped a ground sheet off the floor to show us what he had 'scrounged from under the counter at Steamboat Bill's'. After that, of course, we were so flabbergasted that he had to be forgiven at once. The menu was practically all pre-war: pineapple juice, pork and tomato loaf chopped up and spread with sweet corn, real tinned butter and Swiss Gruyère in triangles of silver paper, and – best of all – California peaches. Only my tummy has since objected.

Further rummaging in the debris of the cowshed above has brought to light tins of sliced turkey (for Thanksgiving?), tomato juice, coffee powder, boiled sweets, chewing-gum, and what would be at least a year's ration of sugar for one person at home. There are heaps of K rations of the *Breakfast, Dinner* and *Supper* varieties, consisting mainly of various unsatisfying-looking compressed foods called 'meat products' and 'fruit bars', plus more chewing-gum, cigarettes and – most thoughtful – in the *Breakfast* containers a dozen folded sheets of lav. paper. I have also acquired a musty-smelling waterproof jerkin, with a brown lambswool collar, and a pair of felt gloves, but I have a sneaking feeling that they may have belonged to some dead person. There are so many odds and ends, personal kit, etc., in the cowshed, that my impression is that, whenever anyone was killed, those of his belongings that were considered to be of no further value were chucked up there with the rest of the rubbish. Why, otherwise, do we find things like wallets and razors? I have kept for myself a souvenir medal, obviously 'struck' by some enterprising Neapolitan, with a relief of Vesuvius on one side, and on the other: 'Welcome gallant soldier, ally of Italia. 1943.' A large variety of picture postcards are scattered about, including some rather titillating ones from Pompei; two cards I have picked out show views of peacetime Anzio, both night scenes of illuminated lidos built on stilts over the sea, with rowing-boats and smart yachts moored all round.

I stopped writing to look outside, as I had heard the sound of an explosion, quite near.

A herd of white cattle, the sort with the giant horns, had come wandering to the front, and one of them had stepped on a mine. By the time I had pulled myself out of the fox-hole, all the other animals were careering madly in every direction. Two more went on to our minefield, and I saw the flash and puff of smoke as they went up. No doubt the Germans were also watching, and they will now have noted where not to send their patrols.

The whole of this area is strewn with the bodies of cattle, sheep and horses, killed by mines or blast from shells. When you get close to them, the smell is pretty bad and I expect it will get a deal niftier when the hot weather comes (this has been an exceptionally cold winter, but the Italian March – says Bishop – is often unpredictable, and the people call it the mad child month). Tonight, if there's time and I can spare the men, I'll send out a burial squad.

25th March

Last night was more energetic than I had bargained for. Having already paid my routine visit to Stonk Corner (called, incidentally, San Lorenzo on the map), I was ordered there again at about midnight by Major Babworth over the wireless; he wanted to tell me about some new change in the Battalion front. An hour later along came another summons, with a further change of plan.

The upshot of all this to-ing and fro-ing is that my platoon is to be much more concentrated on this cowshed, and my particular preoccupation will now be the slight gully that leads straight from here across the fields towards the Jerry lines – the only covered line of approach for some distance round. Tonight we must make a start on digging the new trenches.

The moon was late coming up, and on each of my trips to Stonk Corner I lost my way, on the second occasion jolly nearly getting shot up by a sentry. We also had our first casualty, from shrapnel. It was Whelen who was hit – a pukka funk if ever there was one. He insisted that he was a stretcher-case, and in the end, as every spare member of the platoon was at a bren post, Bishop and I

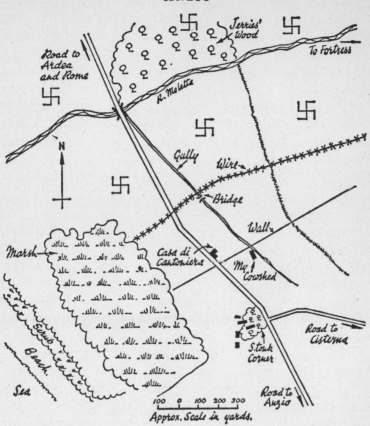

had to carry him. This time the new moon was showing, but not enough to stop me from tripping over some farm implement. Whelen was flung from the stretcher, and let out such a caterwaul as must have chilled the blood of everyone, Germans included, within half a mile of us.

On our return journey Bishop and I had to lay down a telephone wire, and then fix up connections to various key outposts. Ammo had to be checked, and grouses listened

35

to. One section had been using Yankee blankets, which were full of lice. Another complained about the dead sheep, and a man tried to go sick because he was suffering from nausea. At least two bren posts had seen movement on skylines and demanded that trip-flares should be laid – out of the question until I had been given a chart of the minefield.

Meanwhile Sergeant Chesterton was sorting out the rations; every man had to be issued with his share before light. Major Babworth had given me some vague instruction about our having to supply food to a section from the Carrier Platoon, acting as another bren post by the Jerry wire on the road to our left. Nobody knew exactly where these fellows were, and all Major B. could say was that I would have to keep my 'bloody eyes peeled', as the Jerries themselves kept a listening post along there as well, quite possibly on our side of the wire. Needless to say, Bishop and I were the only two available in the platoon for the job.

We stuffed our pockets with grenades, and set off with tommy-guns at the alert. There was no difficulty in finding the road, which was lined with oleander bushes, five or six yards apart. The moon was now rising and these bushes afforded the only cover. We dodged from one to the other, each time stopping a moment to listen. It was a curse having to act so stealthily as we knew that the Carrier Platoon was composed of old sweats, notoriously trigger-happy.

We must have passed at least a dozen oleander bushes, when Bishop tripped and fell against me, sending my tommy-gun clattering on to the hard surface of the road. We didn't at first dare stir an inch, and there wasn't long to wait. As soon as we heard the familiar cork-popping sound farther down the road, we knew that the Jerry two-inch mortars were opening up.

For protection we had to rely on the only available ditch, scarcely more than an indentation in the turf. Bishop had flung himself down some ten yards away from me. Each time I heard the thin overhead whistle of the approaching bomb, I expected the worst, and my whole body screwed up in an effort to hug the ground more closely. But the bombs were not very powerful, and most turned out to be duds. They appeared to be falling all round us, some a couple of dozen yards away.

The last bomb of all had a different whistle to the rest. This is it, I thought; here goes, chum. I became absolutely limp. And the bomb fell slap between Bishop and me, a matter of three feet from where I was lying. But the thing was a dud, and I could hear the red-hot metal sizzling. . . .

28th March

All the last nights have been spent digging. My palms are so blistered that I have had to wrap handkerchiefs round them when I was working, and my shirt is all cardboardy with sweat. Many of the men in my platoon happen to be miners, and whenever they grumble I take pleasure in reminding them of this fact. But they are a good friendly lot on the whole.

We still suffer from a water shortage and I have not washed properly, still less shaved, since our arrival. I brought my face flannel in my pack, but it's only fit now for swabbing the floor of the foxhole.

The Germans can't fail to have heard us at work with our picks, for the ground is stony below the surface. I keep urging everyone that this makes it all the more important that we should finish off our new dugouts as quickly as possible. In our half-prepared positions we are far more vulnerable than when we arrived. The Yanks left us three Browning machine-guns and these I am siting along the wall, in such a way that anyone crossing the field ahead of us from the Jerry lines would have very moderate prospects of survival indeed.

I am frankly amazed that we haven't been stonked more often. Rumour has it that a Panzer division is taking over the wood in front, and so our friends there may be temporarily preoccupied. But Panzers generally mean trouble in the end. Other platoons of ours have been attacked by the odd patrol. There was a considerable shindy over to our right at 2 a.m. today, and the Jerry officer was killed (he was baron or something).

Every morning before light comes we have to spend a good hour camouflaging the freshly turned-up earthheaps. Most of the new section dugouts are now proof against blast or shrapnel, but we don't want to advertise for a stonking. My aim is to operate two sets of trenches: one for night observation, the other for 'kip' or sleeping in by day. Our most important post, indeed almost the *raison d'être* of our being here, is next to a crumbling brick bridge at the end of the gully, right against the wire. Here slit-trenches have already been provided for us by the Americans; a section occupies them by night, withdrawing again at dawn. Viner belongs to the section at present manning this forward post. When he called in here last night to collect the rations, he was obviously wistful at being denied the cushiness of H.Q. – the first glimmer of expression that he has ever displayed in all the weeks that I have been at close quarters with him.

I am also constructing crawl trenches up to the wall so that I can reach any of the section areas by day. These, too, are nearly finished, but using them has made the skin on my knees terribly sore. I am determined that from now onwards we shall be *offensive*, and I am planning all sorts of ambushes and snipers' hideouts. One of the troubles at the Fortress, I'm convinced, was that we allowed the

Germans to feel that they had the upper hand. It's no use meekly sitting back, waiting to have your brains blown out. Now I have a peppering-up policy, and just for the hell of it send a few mortar shells over into the wood, at the same time belting off a dozen rounds from the Brownings and brens. At least by doing this we ensure that the weapons are kept in working order. . . .

Adrian has gone down with malaria, after the last 'duffy' at the Fortress (this battalion almost has a language of its own – it's worse than Winchester notions). That means that Percy Mendelvine, or Mepacrine as we always used to call him in Algiers, is the only one of my original friends left. He calls in here, sometimes several times a night, and we wax sentimental about Le Bosphore and the Aletti. He has got the job of liaising with a bunch of Yanks who are spotting for artillery from an upper floor of one of the houses still standing (partly anyhow) at Stonk Corner – not always an enviable perch, with those Jerry shells whirling over. The Yanks have a tremendously high-powered telescope and Mepacrine says that they have great sport directing fire on to concentrations of vehicles, etc. What's more, he says there is a considerable amount of movement going on along the river-bed in front of my wood, easily visible with field glasses. So I have applied for a telescopic sniper's rifle. . . .

We couldn't for a long while discover the source of a most pungent whiff of animal putrefaction, that hung like a screen over the gully every time we went up to the forward post. It was Sergeant Chesterton who tracked it down to an artificial cave in which an enormous white bull had been barricaded up. No doubt the creature had belonged to the farmer of Stonk Corner, and he – assuming that the Allied landings in January were but the prelude to a swift drive on Rome – had hastily hidden away what must have been one of his most valued possessions.

39

It's horrid to think of it dying slowly of starvation in there. Little did the farmer imagine that not only he and his family, but the entire population of Anzio and Nettuno would be evacuated. There are a few shepherds left, but these are now the only civilians in the entire Beachhead – and even they are going to be shipped back to Naples, as some are accused of acting as spies for the enemy. But most of the cattle run loose, wholly uncared for. We have buried as many of the bodies round here as we can, but some are on the minefield and inaccessible; they lie like swollen waterskins, with purple match-sticks for legs. It is said the Germans often drive flocks of sheep on to the minefields in order to clear the way for an attack.

A starved tabby, so thin and covered with bald patches that it looks like the reincarnation of one of the mummified Egyptian cats in the British Museum, inhabits the cowshed above us. Absolutely crazed by the noise, it refuses to budge. We leave out what food we can, but hardly anything is touched. *I am thy soul, Nikoptis.* Often enough we stumble over it in the dark; the un-initiated who do this are so startled that they think they have detonated a booby-trap.

Squash and Sergeant Chesterton have been busy reorganizing the *décor* of the foxhole, and have made shelves out of Yankee ration boxes. Polished mess-tins and some chipped china cups hang in rows on bent nails, and the sergeant has made paraffin lamps out of cigarette tins with pieces of four-by-two as wicks. These lamps send up coils of sooty smoke, and you expect hideous ear-ringed djinns to come menacing out of them; they also have the effect of making our faces and hair filthier than ever.

Another legacy from the Americans is a selection of pin-ups, of the Ziegfeld Follies type, which have duly been put up on our walls by Squash. He says that they do the soul good and make the place more homey. When we

40

have had enough of his gloating over them, we remind him of his old woman, who by all accounts would be the very last to tolerate ostrich-feather-clad floozies lolling around in the home. This shuts him up so effectively that he becomes tearful, involving apologies all round.

Bishop affects to be entirely uninterested in the pin-ups. He comes from Romney Marsh and is an *aficionado* for fishing. In fact, he says that he would never need to look at a girl as he is already married to his fish. His other subject is politics and he ties poor Squash up into knots, about why we are at war and the working man's prospects afterwards. His eyes have a colourless transparent look, as though from staring too long at water. The rest of his features are all scraggy – scraggy nose and chin, scraggy locks of hair falling over his forehead, and a scraggy broken tooth, which he uses as a cigarette-holder. We tell him he smokes too much. All his cigarettes have to be rolled 'by hand', and if you offer him one he will take out the tobacco and re-wrap it in his own paper.

To complete the picture of my three bedfellows, I should say something about Sergeant Chesterton. He is a regular soldier, I suppose in his late thirties (Bishop, by the way, is twenty-eight), red-faced, with a shock of grey hair, a Clark Gable moustache and heavy dark eyebrows that give him the air of a broken-down clown. Unlike most other N.C.O.s who have been with the Battalion since Catania, he is not the least bit bomb-happy and positively revels in situations that cause the maximum amount of jitters in other people. Yet, when somebody in the platoon is seriously wounded or has had distressing news from home, I have seen him behave with the utmost tenderness. We all regard him as a jolly knockabout parent, but it needs a certain amount of psychology to know when he is being sarcastic or deadly earnest – to make a mistake can be disastrous. He has a son, I have discovered, only three years younger than myself – a fact which I have not disclosed to him.

Sergeant Chesterton's main hobby is loot. He wears a gold watch that he took from a Jerry he shot at Minturno, and he boasts that, back at Naples, he has trunkfuls of bottles of scent, rolls of silk, plates of solid silver, cameos and more gold watches. He persuaded me last night to join him on a looting party to one of the more intact houses at Stonk Corner. The plan was to find some proper furniture for our foxhole, perhaps a chair or two. But the house had already been stripped bare. Apart from two old iron bedsteads, a mouse-eaten mattress, and some broken Chianti bottles, the only things of value were a dozen twenty-bore cartridges – useless without a gun, which is a shame as Mepacrine says that there are duck on the marsh. . . .

Major Babworth has gone on leave, and we have another company commander. He departs with my blessing. Tonight I'll see if the new régime can't rustle up some more A.L. 63 powder. The meagre allowance we had before hasn't been nearly enough to cope with the lice that plague us all. We in Platoon H.Q. are not so badly affected, although Sergeant Chesterton has cast doubts on the straw in the doss-house. No. 3 section, the one that had the American blankets, say that they are covered with rashes and that their legs are so chafed they can't sleep. I am also hoping to scrounge a proper hurricane lamp.

29th March

This morning, when the men from the forward post by the bridge had withdrawn to their day positions, old Ma Baxter came puffing along the crawl trench, all googly eye-balls. Both Viner and Corporal Pye had disappeared during the night. The whole thing is a complete mystery, as none of the trenches up there are more than five yards away from one another. We can't believe that a Jerry patrol could have pinched them without Baxter and the rest hearing something. Surely the two of them can't have *bolted*? The very thought is so heretical that I wish I could write it in a whisper. The Jerry wire up there is supposed to be heavily booby-trapped. One could expect anything from Viner with that dead-pan mask of his, but Corporal Pye is a dear little man, like a fuzzy gnome. Sergeant Chesterton says that he himself will spend the night at the forward post and at the same time check the wire for breakages. There will be hell to pay when I report this to the new pocket-sized company commander, Jim Eagle, who is desperately keen (*'We'll* get the whiphand over Jerry') and anxious to assert himself, albeit toothy and old-maidish with his red wavy hair. He is driving us all dotty by insisting that we must get a prisoner soon, now that we have a Panzer division in front of us. What has made matters worse is that last night a Jerry patrol sneaked in ('Cheeky devils, my word') and set fire to a hayrick only a stone's throw from Company H.Q., lately removed from Stonk Corner.

One piece of improvement in our living conditions is that I have found a stagnant pool in the middle of the field behind us. That means we can wash and shave, even though the water is full of wriggling larvae. Sergeant Chesterton turns out to be covered with tattoo marks. He is very proud of them, particularly of the cobras twisted round his biceps. On his right forearm he has a tombstone, with MOTHER written on it, and all over his front there is an enormous fire-breathing dragon, cleverly incorporating the hair on his chest into the design, and with his nipples for eyes.

43

Bishop tells us that we all shave in the wrong way. He claims to be an artist in shaving. Half the trick is to take enough trouble with the lather, but to make your blade last you must use long strokes instead of short jabs. All his best thoughts of the day come to him when he is shaving. On hearing this, Squash has proposed that we should observe a two-minute silence every time Bishop shaves in future.

Rhinology, or the science of blowing your nose properly, is another 'subject' of Bishop's. Blow steadily, gently, and you won't break a blood-vessel.

Corporal Peter came to collect some A.L. 63 during the night. He smelt very bad, like a stale dairy. I thought he must have stepped on a dead sheep, or that he had been somehow affected by the lice. But Sergeant Chesterton says that he is always like this, even after a bath. The wretched fellow has been so worried by it all that on several occasions he has been to consult the M.O.

30th March

The plot thickens. Apparently Viner and Corporal Pye both took with them not only their small packs, containing mess-tins and washing kit, but a quantity of conner and compôt as well. (One would have thought that they'd have welcomed a change of diet, wherever they were going!) Yet Viner left a trail of his belongings up to a break in the wire, so we have no doubt now that that's where they got through. The sergeant, as I write, is busily preparing his own special brand of booby-traps, or ****
ticklers, for stringing up along there tonight.

Jim Eagle was very snappy when I suggested that we must take into account the possibility that Viner and Pye might have deserted. 'Then you obviously think you've

44

lost the confidence of your men,' he retorted. Luckily the debonair C.S.M., always an ally of mine, was there to smooth things out.

Partly inspired by Mepacrine's accounts of what he sees from his Stonk Corner perch, and partly to pacify Jim Eagle, I have been doing some solo daylight patrolling. I went this morning to a ruined *Casa di Cantoniera*, or roadmender's house, not far from where the Carrier Platoon used to have their bren post. There is a theory that the Jerries hide up there by night, purely for observation. By day it is stonked occasionally, but in a half-hearted manner.

I found the place in a shambles, with most of the ceilings collapsed, but I could still pull myself up to the first floor. Evidently it had been in recent occupation by the Yanks, judging by the heaps of K rations and oddments of clothing and ammo everywhere. Downstairs was no less than an open latrine, and there were obscene drawings all over the walls.

Although I didn't spot any movement through my glasses, I distinctly saw three large sets of earthworks in front of the wood. These should interest our mortars. . . .

31st March

So now we know. That idiot Baxter only told me half the story about Viner and Corporal Pye. It appears that just before dawn, on the morning they disappeared, Baxter heard whispering and tins clattering from their direction. He was going to tell them to pipe down, and had already started to crawl over when he saw against the sky the large shape of a man, bending over their trench – he remembers that the shape seemed bigger than Viner or Pye, who are in any case below average size. As soon as the man saw

45

him coming, he at once jumped into the trench. The noise stopped immediately, so Baxter went back without saying anything.

We now assume that Viner, contrary to all rules, must have gone to sleep and attracted a Jerry patrol by his snores. Corporal Pye is deaf in one ear and so he may not have heard them creeping up. Forty-eight hours have gone by since then, and thanks to Baxter all sorts of things might have happened. The Jerries are supposed to use third degree on their prisoners (although, as the sergeant says, they would be unlikely to strike a spark out of Viner), but what is more serious is that they can't fail to have heard our digging party, including myself, seventy yards off. That means we should consider scrapping the new dugouts and building entirely fresh ones elsewhere. After the physical strain of the last nights, I don't fancy the men would stand it.

Two tommy-guns are also reported missing. Corporal Peters swears that they were left on the grass near where his section was digging. When he came to look for them before stand-to at dawn, they had gone. Looks as if I shall have to do another solo patrol to the *Casa di Cantoniera*, if I am to keep Jim Eagle calm. Sergeant Chesterton says that this new broom act at Company H.Q. is passing the limit – passwords, kit inspections, dubbined boots. They call Jim Eagle Righty-O behind his back; he is apparently incapable of using the word 'yes'.

1st April

Since Baxter's revelation the chaps in the forward post have become jumpy. Useless to point out that the break in the wire has been mended as well as booby-trapped by Sergeant Chesterton. What about those missing tommy-guns, they ask? I have agreed that the moment there is a likelihood of attack by the Jerries, they should withdraw at once to the main positions by the wall.

Baxter came along to Platoon H.Q. last night and burst into tears. He said that he had known all along that Viner and Pye had been put in the bag and that the giant shape bending over their trench had been a Jerry. . . .

No less than thirty letters arrived for me yesterday, all forwarded from Algiers and some two months old. I also had two parcels, one containing a tin of Balkan Sobranies and the other a pullover from White's. Now that the weather is so much better, the latter parcel is not of so much use. But – oh, the smell of good London shops! I hardly dared touch the pullover in case I dirtied it. Suddenly I had a vision of a certain Sunday afternoon at York, and I thought of Marigold, La Belle Moule Sans Merci, in pearls and blue cardigan changing a record with blood-red talons. I had to write to her at once. My dear, you should see my *hands*.

Bishop is always particularly interested in the letters I have from Jay [my brother at Winchester], and I have to read out the extracts about catapulting rocks or poaching pike and eels in Water Meads. It is now claimed by Squash that we have heard Bishop's repertoire of fishing stories twice over, and he begged me privately this morning, when Bishop was asleep, not to let it be known when any more letters come from Jay. I barely restrained myself from saying that equally I am bored potty by Squash's tales of lorry-drivers at Steamboat Bill's (Nipper Pat, Alfie, Tiny – we know them all too well), let alone any mention of his old woman's varicose veins.

What does get me down about Bishop is his method of smoking. After each puff he gives a little spit, as if he had some tobacco in his mouth. I find myself watching for the sound and almost making it for him. . . .

A letter has also come from Toumi, recovering from

47

scabies at Bari. He went to a G.I. concert to see Marlene Dietrich. All she had to do was to come on to the stage, hitch her skirt above her knee, and say 'Hallo' in that wonderful husky voice, and there was such an uproar of clapping and catcalls that it was a good ten minutes before she could be heard. 'Falling in Love Again'. Oh, my God.

Toumi is string-pulling hard to get me back to my own regiment as soon as I leave Anzio. Any likely-looking brigadier from A.F.H.Q., who dares set foot in a Bari night-club, is forced to take down my name and number. (I haven't yet mentioned in this diary that I don't 'belong' here, and that – much to my fury *at the time* – I was seconded away from my regiment back in February in order to come to this Beachhead.) Quite honestly, by the time the present duffy is over, all I shall want is a jolly good laze on Capri. When we sailed for Anzio, we were told that six weeks was to be our limit here, but at this rate we may hang on for months yet. Added to that, I'm not sure if my ties with the blokes in this platoon don't outweigh any nebulous loyalty I may have felt towards the traditions of the regiment.

When I originally joined up, straight from school and therefore impressionable, I had it dinned into me day and night that I now belonged to a crack regiment; only Guards regiments and one or two others in the Cavalry could be tolerated. As soon as I went abroad, what happened? Without the smallest apology I and a lot of my contemporaries were doled out as cannon-fodder to any mob that happened to be short of platoon commanders. No wonder at first we were very unhappy, and no wonder now we are bitter with the people who taught us that iniquitous rubbish.

Mepacrine keeps on urging me to call on him some evening at Stonk Corner. He says that his American

48

friends brew the most delicious coffee. But I haven't the energy after all that digging, even though his insistence makes me feel that I'm committing a social blob by not going there.

6th April

For a long time it has been quiet – too quiet, we suspect. We have had plenty of alerts, scares of attack, rumours (via Mepacrine) of troops massing behind the wood, not to mention mortar 'duels', but somehow my platoon has been spared excitement since Viner and Corporal Pye disappeared. The only real shock was a heavy shell that exploded outside the entrance to our foxhole. We were having breakfast at the time (cocoa and fried pork loaf), when there was an almighty shudder and quantities of earth came vomiting down the entrance funnel on to Sergeant Chesterton's tidy floor. Squash's poor old legs became unusually agile and he was through the hatch well before my own reflexes had even begun to sort themselves out. But the only damage was to some sandbags, and there was a messy crater just where I was sunbathing yesterday. None of us heard the shell coming, so the adage that you never hear the one that hits you must be true.

Stonk Corner gets its periodic bashings, and so does my *Casa di Cantoniera*, once when I was in it. Another of the Jerries' favourite targets is a large Martello tower affair on the sand-dunes. I imagine that it was built against the Saracens, perhaps Barbarossa. Most of the shots are misses, but the walls of the tower are so solid that hits hardly make any impression.

I pay frequent visits to the *Casa di Cantoniera* now, sometimes twice a day. Not that I ever seem to get hold of any information that pleases Jim Eagle. I go there mainly to escape – from the toe-jam suffocation of the doss-house,

49

from Bishop's spitting, from the old woman's veins, from myself, the miserable sweaty pallid earth-worm that I have become. The whole of a side of one room on the upper floor of the *Casa di Cantoniera* has been knocked away by a shell, and the farther corner is so sheltered that I can sit there with my shirt off re-reading letters, or if I wish, daydreaming about sentimental things. Near the same corner there is a window that gives me a view over the dunes to the sea, sometimes with waves all chromium in the bright Italian light, sometimes a dead fish English Channel colour. I find it more and more of an effort to force myself to my lookout post. Once I am there, however, and searching the motionless (invariably) enemy lines through my glasses, often I slip into a different sort of daydream – more heroic this time, such as creeping up to the wood in broad daylight when the Jerries would least be expecting me, knifing a few sentries and blowing up a vital ammunition dump or two. A less violent variation is a long-distance patrol to the other side of the wood where I would lie up all day making sketch-maps and noting down the makes of vehicles and weapons; then on my return, twenty-four hours later, I would be congratulated by a Russian observer, who happened to be visiting H.Q. at the time.

But, as we know, the better part of valour. . . . There's much to be said for outliving this war, and I for one feel it all the more strongly after a horrid little drama last night. Actually, it started the night before last: a driver of a 15-cwt. took the wrong turning at Stonk Corner and went tearing down the road past the *Casa di Cantoniera* until he was brought to a full stop at the wire. Before he could turn the Jerry mortars got going and he had to escape on foot. However, he insisted that he could still rescue the truck and went back to fetch it the following night – last night. Of course the Jerries were waiting for him, and they shot him up with schmeissers. He was wounded and ran into the field in front of us, and on to a mine. At least the Jerries did have the heart to put him out of his pain.

Under pressure from Squash the foxhole has now been christened Steamboat Bill's. He even put a placard to this effect outside our entrance, until Jim Eagle spotted it. 'Do you bloody well want a Jerry patrol to go lobbing a grenade down there? Why not call yourselves Piccadilly Circus and advertise Guinness in coloured lights?' We certainly have become a social centre these evenings. Squash and the sergeant have made two benches, seating eight, and anyone who passes drops in for a cuppa, which Sergeant Chesterton 'mashes off'. Thank God, the water situation has much improved; we have become so bold in this sector with lack of activity that a jeep drives up nightly to Company H.Q. with water tins and dixies of fresh stew. The Colour Sergeant is an honorary member of Steamboat Bill's – chief bottle-washer – so we have an extra allocation of compôt tea. Mepacrine and his runner, known as Benzedrine (the two Pills), are always dropping in for a liaison chat, and generally any patrol going forward through our lines visits us first for 'griff'.

But the biggest draw of all is our 38 wireless set, which easily picks up what the Germans call their *Front-Line Radio*, every evening from eleven o'clock onwards. The announcer is a woman who calls herself Sally. She has a bedroomy American accent, and always opens with: 'Hall-o, boys, here's your girl-friend Sall-y. Would you like some boogie-woogie to cheer you up in your lone-ly foxholes?' We then listen to a couple of very worn records – you can actually hear the needles scraping on them – at the end of which Sally heaves a sigh, and says: 'Gee, that was *good*. Now for some news from your pals back here safe with Jerry.' She reads out a list of names, purporting to be those of the latest G.I.s to be taken prisoner by the Germans, and ends up with some 'messages' about the scrumptious food and gentle treatment we can expect if only we throw down our arms and go over to the other side. Then follows: 'And now, here is some news from your Limey friends.' More names (but never Viner or Corporal Pye) and some studiously authentic message, often ending with the word Mizpah or T.T.F.N. (Ta-ta for now.) First prize goes to an effort, supposed to be from an officer in this very battalion (a name quite unknown to us, needless to say): 'I say chaps, it's jolly decent here,' all repeated slowly and with Teutonic earnestness in an American accent. Finally Sally says: 'Think it over, boys. Why not join Jerry too, and get away from those goddam foxholes? Come and meet *me*—' (seductive whisper); 'Sall-y.' At that a man's voice chimes in, again with an American accent, but rather more guttural this time: 'Aw, stow it, Sal. Let's have some more music.' So boogie-woogie, etc., again, even 'In the Mood' and 'Chattanooga-Choo-Choo'. Each record is followed by a news item about Russians retreating, London under bombardment, or the impending withdrawal from Cassino by the Allies. As for the Second Front, it's amazing that Winston and Eisenhower haven't given up the idea months ago. Sometimes we are treated to a choice grisly tale: 'Have you heard about Private Fox? He went on patrol and stepped on a shoe-mine. Nasty things, shoe-mines. All his guts were blown away. But he went on living another twelve hours. You should have heard him yelling out,' etc., etc. The programme always ends with the man saying: 'Well, so long, folks. That's the end of today's programme. Don't forget to listen in to Jerry's Front-Line Radio again tomorrow. And think it over. Why should *you* be one of those rotting carcasses?' 'And a big kiss from Sall-y.'

I'm told that the Germans used amplifiers at the Fortress for relaying their Front-Line Radio, until our people used the noise as cover for a patrol.

Yesterday we were baffled at first by some German rockets, which exploded with a plop in the air above us. There was no shrapnel, and we knew that they were not lethal. Only when daylight came did we discover that they had contained leaflets, all of particularly crude and childishly horrific nature. One shows Neptune (Nettuno) holding squirming British and American soldiers on his trident, with the caption: 'The beaches of Nettuno and Anzio are strewn with Allied corpses. YOU WILL BE THE NEXT.' Another gives us a picture of the half-decayed body of a G.I., sprawled grotesquely near a broken tree in a Retreat from Mons landscape, and the caption this time is: 'Most of you believe that the war will be over in a few months. Too bad if you should be hit at the last minute.'

(*Do* we believe that the war will be over in a few months? I call this one encouraging.)

The other type of leaflet is anti-American. For instance, a woman in a petticoat is shown sitting on a crumpled bed as she pulls on a stocking, whilst a G.I. straightens his tie in front of the mirror. The caption for this is: 'What goes on at home whilst you are away. No woman can resist such handsome brutes from the wide open spaces.' Then there is another, entitled 'You Americans are soooo wonderful', showing two abandoned un-British-looking *hausfrauen* hanging round a G.I's neck.

I caught Squash sending home a selection of these leaflets. He was putting them in a blue-triangle envelope (therefore not liable to be opened by the censor). I tried to stop him in case the horror ones would give the wrong impression to his old woman; if she and her friends belong to the same mental stratum as Squash, these leaflets are just the things to cause alarm. But Squash became all snarly and defensive, and in the end I had to give way, if only because of the sheer boredom of having to be involved in an argument with a brick wall.

Banal and crashingly stupid though all this propaganda is, there's no doubt that it's having an effect on the likes of Squash, who seems to have lost all his bounce recently. Gone are the tales, bawdy or otherwise, about the original Steamboat Bill's. Nowadays it's nothing but grouse, grouse, grouse. Why are we here at all at Anzio? Why don't we get a move on, or clear out? What's the use of wasting men, wasting money? 'I don't want to kill a Tedeschi, any more than he wants to kill me.' Blah, blah.

This boredom does get you down, and there's no doubt that one's nerves are worn thin by the mere lack of news and the nagging feeling all the time that something is brewing up. We do nothing but watch and wait. Stag comes at dusk, and again at dawn. Twice a day we expect the attack that never materializes. Our weapons are cocked, our eyes strain into the twilight; the slightest gust of wind causes palpitations. It will be a relief to be in danger again. Sergeant Chesterton says that we must keep Squash under observation; he shows all the symptoms of the first stages of bomb-happiness. . . .

Sergeant Chesterton himself is temporarily to leave us and to take over the command of the neighbouring platoon. In ten days' time he is also going on leave, to Sorrento and Amalfi. Bishop is leaving me for a mortar course at Nettuno. It will be sad to have our quartet broken up. I am worried about all those men being taken from me. To send people *from the front line* on leave, courses, even court-martials, seems utterly crazy. . . .

Winter has really left us now. Mosquitoes hover in clouds round the entrance to Steamboat Bill's, as if it were a filthy cesspool. We have also been discovered by ants, which laboriously trundle away the crumbs left from the

54

cheese sandwiches at tiffin time. Over the minefield, in the field between us and the Germans, lupins are beginning to spring up; it would be nice to have a bunch in the fox-hole; they remind me of that famous occasion on trek across the Borzil Pass in Kashmir, when Mother beat me for walking in the snow to pick denticulatas.

Frogs make a great row in the marsh and up the gully by the bridge. I hadn't even heard frogs croaking like that before, and at first I was puzzled to make out whether they were nightjars or some peculiarly garrulous type of duck, afflicted by chronic insomnia. Some lines from 'The Fairies', the first poem I ever learnt, kept coming up in my mind:

> *Down along the rocky shore*
> *Some make their home,*
> *They live on crispy pancakes*
> *Of yellow tide-foam;*
>
> *Some in the reeds*
> *Of the black mountain lake,*
> *With frogs for their watch-dogs,*
> *All night awake.*

For these frogs certainly are our watch-dogs. Immediately they hear anyone coming, they stop croaking. On a number of occasions they have warned us of Jerry marauders.

There are owls here, too; some perch on the roof of the cowshed. They give Squash the creeps, he says. But to me they bring back memories of Kennedy's Eating Brimer – *strix, strigis*, himself in person at last.

The tabby cat, Elsie, came to grief yesterday after trying to catch one of the owls. We couldn't think what all the uproar was about, the yowling and the fluttering. In

55

the morning we found Elsie's body, terribly lacerated, sans eyes.

We have also made efforts to tame lizards, but they don't respond and *will* shed their tails the moment we touch them. One, living in the wall above Steamboat Bill's, has warts.

In a fit of hating myself I wrote a long depressing letter to Toumi, and afterwards felt much better. He'd soon brighten us up – only this place would have to be called the Juke Box, not Steamboat Bill's, and instead of gooey compôt tea out of mess-tins we would be having 'sippikins' from his cocktail shaker. I've never known Toumi to have blackers, and he never allowed anyone else to have them either. However gloom-making the circumstances – a cattle truck (*hommes* 40: *chevaux* 8) jogging through snow in the Little Atlas, a leaky tent at Foggia, a Nissen hut full of hostile majors at Retford – he always had the answer: the Juke Box. Out came the cocktail shaker; garish Wog cushions were shaken up and fur-lined coats thrown in careless heaps; then Toumi would produce some miraculous drop of gin or cognac that somehow he'd managed to preserve, and he would mix it up with anything that had taste, even toothpaste, provided it wasn't actually poisonous. Later, as we began to warm up, he would treat us to an exhibition of Ouëd Naîl stomach dancing or one of Frances Day's latest numbers.

Reading hopelessly behind. I have picked about in *War and Peace* and have now swopped it for Boswell's *Johnson*, belonging to our new second-in-command. 'For God's sake, no literary swooning parties while I'm around,' said Jim Eagle, when he saw us doing the exchange. But he needn't worry, as I can't even concentrate on Boswell. The Colour Sergeant brings us copies of the *Union Jack* most nights – that's about as much as I can manage.

Today, I'd almost forgotten, is my parents' wedding anniversary. . . .

The Americans left us a Winchester carbine, blessedly light after a tommy-gun, and I take it with me to the *Casa di Cantoniera* in the hope of doing a spot of sniping. Last night Bishop and I went on a 'private' patrol, more to enjoy a whiff of night air and to avoid Sally than anything else. Our excuse was that we were going to check up on breaks in the wire. There was a warm breeze blowing from the sea and the sky was glittering with stars. We never, in fact, got as far as the wire, but lay down on our backs half-way up the gully trying to pick out Orion and the Pleiades. Suddenly several Jerry planes streaked over towards the port, evidently making for the convoy that arrived there yesterday. Our ack-ack started up, and we were treated to a fireworks display on the grand scale. The whole sky was spattered with Roman candles, squibs, rockets, and cascades of luminous midges. We felt unaccountably exhilarated and I thought: *The morning stars sang together, and all the sons of God shouted for joy.*

One of the aeroplanes was hit; yellow and scarlet tongues fled out from it like a portent. Although the pilot managed to get back to the Jerry lines, the plane crashed and blew up with a roar that made the whole ground tremble. This disaster seemed to scare away all the other Jerry planes. We have had a series of these raids recently. Rumour has it that the *Penelope* (Squash pronounces it Pean-loop, and refuses to be corrected) was sunk in the harbour not long ago.

8th April

More pi-jaws from Jim Eagle about the consequences of our not being able to secure a prisoner. He says that it is vital that we should know more about the goings on in the

57

Jerries' wood, especially now that we have been hearing tanks there. In fact he went so far as to detail me for a patrol up to the wood, for the very purpose of nabbing a prisoner. I had only myself to blame, after shooting all those lines about the *Casa di Cantoniera* – more so, if Jim E. were capable of mind-reading! What a coward one can become when faced with realities! That patrol meant crawling through the booby-trapped wire, over a ridge and therefore in full view under the gibbous moon. Then there would have been the Jerry minefield to reckon with.

It was Sergeant Chesterton who saved me from the patrol. Although now commanding 16 Platoon, he still regards himself as our official godfather. He was so indignant when he heard about the scheme, that he went himself to Jim Eagle and offered to take my place. This – along with a timely oar put in by my friend the C.S.M. – proved effective, and Jim unexpectedly relented. Now he has devised a new plan: we are to set an ambush by deliberately making a break in the wire; I am to leave a section nearby, and they are to lie up until the Jerries discover the break and send a patrol through.

It was the minefield of which I was frightened. I don't mind a fighting chance, but I have a dread of mines.

Life at Steamboat's is not what it used to be. Squash has become very edgy, mumbles to himself, and looks bleary and haggard. Sergeant Chesterton and Bishop are both gone. The new sergeant reminds me of a camel; he chews the cud.

Jay will be back at home on his holidays now. Mother writes that the forsythia in front of the house has been better than ever this year; she heard people stopping in the lane, and one saying to the other: 'Oh look. Ain't it out?' She also tells me that she was travelling in a railway compartment recently with a woman and a very restive child, holding a bunch of catkins. Without any warning, the woman gave the child a vicious slap, saying: '*Charley, don't pluck naitcher.*'

Mother would be amused to hear how unconsciously I address Squash and Co. as 'kid' nowadays – so much has my mind become soused with the way they have of talking in this platoon. And of course it always is 'aye' for yes.

Up in the cattle-shed I came across a page torn from an Italian guide-book, dealing with this part of the country. (Why that American should have *torn* out the page, I can't imagine.) How musical and romantic the Italian language can be, even in a guide-book. The next hamlet from here is called Ardea, and you reach it *per una via amena e ombrosa*. The stream in front of the Jerries' wood – the one that eventually leads up to the Fortress – is called the Fossa della Moletta, where *si rasentano pinarelle e grandi fattorie, avvicandosi gradatamente al mare che rimane al lungo nascosto*. The page ends with a reference to the Belvedere Apollo being discovered at Nero's villa outside Anzio. Nero was born at Anzio, so was Caligula.

After Ardea, Rome.

9th April

Easter Sunday, and we had our eggs powdered for breakfast. Waves of nostalgia. Oxlips and early purples in the Hart Wood. Anemones – wind-flowers – at Oak Springs. King's College Chapel. Bicycling in service dress to York Minster. And now I spend the better part of the spring of 1944 beneath a cowshed. For this is our seventeenth day here. I have invited Sergeant Chesterton, Mepacrine and Benzedrine over to Steamboat's tonight, to finish off the last of the Yankee pineapple.

God, how I yearn for a hot bath or – in the Army's

59

polite phrase – a disinfestation. Since I arrived in Italy, now well over two months ago, I have only had one shower.

Jim Eagle announces that it is not worth our while keeping the observation post up by the bridge, so long as we send a patrol to visit it every night. The snag at present is that, the post being so very isolated, there wouldn't be a hope of sending help in time if it were attacked. As a matter of fact, I'm surprised the Jerries haven't already tried to mop it up after the *affaire* Viner/Pye.

10th April

Baxter came to see us at Steamboat's last night, really to gatecrash our party. In the course of conversation I mentioned that I was worried about the shortage of Browning ammo. He then volunteered that there were stacks of it up at the observation post. The dope, why didn't he tell me before? We shall have to fetch it back at once, now that the trenches have been abandoned.

It looks as if Divisional H.Q. expects a real bust-up before long. I now have two twelve-pounders under my command, with their camouflaged muzzles sticking through holes in the wall. There is a general flap about those Jerry tanks massing behind the wood. Certainly the lupin field is ideal country for a tank attack. I wonder if that's why the Jerries have left my platoon alone for so long? Do they hope that we'll become careless and unwatchful?

No. 16 Platoon, on the other hand, has had to beat off frequent sallies by fighting patrols. Sergeant Chesterton says it makes a nice change. Last night he had a dose of Moaning Minnie, a multi-barrelled rocket gun that fires with a weird screech and sends out shells that explode in clouds of phosphorus. Some of 16's men were nastily burnt, but – at last, at last – two Jerry prisoners were taken.

11th April

Yesterday we had to fetch back the Browning ammo from the observation post, so I went up the gully with four men. As we came round the last corner, I could see the arch of the bridge thirty yards off, quite distinctly in the moonlight. I was afraid to go on, and I could sense that the men were faltering too. The frogs were not croaking. Then it happened like this: from the trenches ahead there was a rattle of bolts, a shout – *'Feuer!'* – and a spandau, then two spandaus, opened up at us. I saw red rods darting by me, and the little flames from the barrels of the spandaus.

We doubled back round the corner. I was untouched, but three of the others were wounded, one very badly with a bullet in his neck. The fourth, Jolly – he was nineteen – I think was killed. We haven't yet been able to recover him. Jim Eagle says I must go up there again tonight and re-establish a permanent observation post. It will mean having to lay on a full-scale fighting patrol. And if ever we manage to reach those trenches, what about booby-traps? . . .

THE FORTRESS AGAIN

THE following night I went with the patrol to the end of the gully. We found the trenches deserted, and not even booby-trapped. Jolly's body had also disappeared, so we had no means of telling whether he was still alive. Twenty-four hours later we had left San Lorenzo for good and were back at B Echelon.

After three weeks' interval everything had quite changed there. Not only were the trees and hedges in full leaf, but the back-room boys had been pathetically anxious to prove that they, too, had had their share of toil. New and roomy sleeping-trenches had been dug for us, singles for officers and doubles for O.R.s. I had been provided with a camouflage net for my mattress – too soft after the straw at Steamboat's – and by my bedside was a mahogany chest of drawers with its legs sawn off. Somebody had even given me a little yellow vase, with *Ricordo di Nettuno* on it and containing six wild cyclamen. Everywhere there were signs of large-scale looting; all inhibitions about taking things from civilian houses had evidently been forgotten. Our mess now possessed a table and chairs, not to mention check napkins and some ornate monogrammed plates and cutlery. There was also a bathroom attached, with two full-length enamel baths.

The atmosphere in the mess was very different to the time when we had first come out of the line. There was no cribbage and no hard drinking, even though during our absence our drink ration had accumulated remarkably; each officer found that he had acquired over a dozen bottles of beer, two bottles of sherry, one of gin, and one of whisky, plus rum *ad lib*. In the evenings I would spend much of my time with Simon Waites, the new second-in-command. Talk about the war, and especially our recent doings, was strictly *verboten*, and we would instead reminisce about London plays or the New Forest, where he lived, or discuss Boswell's *Johnson*, which he'd lent me at the Front. Every afternoon we would walk through the pineta to the beach, and lie on the pumice-coloured sand where a space had been cleared in the minefield. The water was still too cold for swimming, and trench warfare had given us such a crop of spots on the behinds that at first we were a bit guarded about sunbathing.

Simon and I were often joined by Monty Muir, a sub-altern who had lately arrived from Naples as a reinforcement for another company. Actually, Monty belonged to my own regiment, although I'd never met him before. Two years older than myself, half-French but not a bit Latin in appearance, stocky and somewhat pasty-complexioned, he had the most staggering vitality. Simon, on whose features – it was true – fatigue seemed to have been indelibly engrained, used to say that Monty made him feel a tired old Chelsea Pensioner (Simon rather enjoyed pretending that he belonged to a different generation to us both). At first Monty's behaviour bewildered the men, but he soon became immensely popular. He would stride about B Echelon twirling a cane as if he were a bandmaster and singing popular songs at the top of his voice, or else humming regimental marches – '*Tara-ti-ta-ta-ta*.' Whenever he spied someone he knew, he would yell out: 'Morning, Corporal, how go the jaded nerves today?' or 'Been down for a dip yet, Figgins?' Baxter, who had now become my batman, would say

63

every night to me: 'Mr. Muir, he's quite a lad, isn't he, sir?'

In some ways Monty reminded me of Toumi. He very rarely allowed himself to be downcast; each minute had to be lived to the full, regardless of the ever-present grumble of distant artillery and the attentions of Anzio Annie, the German long-range gun that was supposed to fire from up by Lake Nemi somewhere. He always seemed to live on the crest of the Present. The only time I ever detected a trace of unhappiness in him was one evening when we were walking through the starlit pineta, and he told me about a girl called Ursula with whom he'd been in love, but who had married somebody else.

Monty also went in for being a great socialite. He knew everyone in London, patronized the Four Hundred, the Orchid Room and the Bagatelle. It turned out that we had some friends in common, so Simon called us Tatler and Bystander. Then one day Monty came into my trench and saw the pocket Keats that I always take with me to the front, and that started a new phase: this was perfect Keats country; Pan was everywhere, hamadryads lurked in the shade, here were naiads, there were the haunts of Syrinx. We might be walking down to the beach, when he would suddenly clutch my arm and hiss: 'Hush, don't move. What was that rustling in the bushes? Can't you smell *goat*?' He would learn pages of *Endymion*, so that he could declaim them as we drove in our jeep among the ruined houses and the dumps of ammunition covered with tarpaulins, dodging the M.P.s who shouted at us because we were not wearing tin hats.

So the days slipped by, and on the night of 18th April Monty, Simon and I were all at the Fortress.

This place is the complete opposite to Steamboat's. We are under constant observation by the enemy during daylight, and dare not lift our heads above the trenches because of snipers. Rifle grenades also keep lobbing over; as we have no chance of retaliating, we can only crouch in our holes and pray for the best.

A shell-marked ridge runs above us, with a slight slope of about thirty yards in between. To our right is a sheer drop into the wadi, on the opposite side of which is my original platoon area, the one I was at when I first came to the Fortress. In fact, my present position is precisely where I saw those Jerries putting down coils of wire on the skyline.

Sergeant Chesterton is on leave, so I share this trench with a new man, Sergeant Denholm. Baxter, as runner, is next door on his own. Then there is a gap of about fifteen yards, and the remainder of the trenches are strung in a line along the edge of the wadi. The first of the trenches is unusable, as it has been made into a communal grave for our casualties. Bishop is in the second; I have tried to press a stripe on him, but he refused it – even so, I have more faith in him than the N.C.O.s to keep control over the others until the sergeant or I can take over.

Much of the scrub round here has been blasted away during the past weeks, and what is left is dead and charred. There is so little green that you would hardly believe that we are nearly into May. The ground is all grey-brown powder and torn up roots. This means that there is less opportunity for Jerry patrols to creep up on us unobserved, and vice versa. The foetid smell of decay is also considerably stronger than it was before.

At the far end of the wadi the Germans keep a spandau, which opens up at haphazard intervals during the day or night. A favourite game of theirs, when it is dark and we are therefore less likely to be below the level of our trenches, is to send over flares, and a few seconds later to rake our area with machine-gun fire, in the hope of catching us standing upright and 'freezing'.

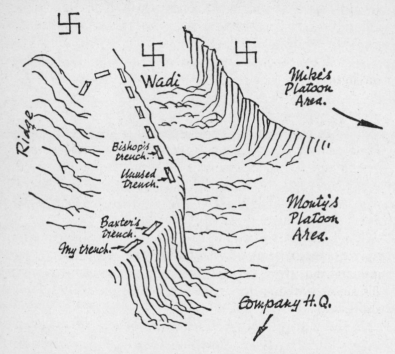

But we are most bothered by the rifle grenades. One man has already been killed, and there have been several narrow misses. It is obvious that the older soldiers are getting shaken again. It is our helplessness that breaks down their nerves: this inability to hit back, and also the fact that a Jerry attack can be almost on top of us before we are aware of it.

Mike Harper now occupies my old platoon area, opposite. I saw him for a few moments when visiting H.Q. last night. He said all the bushes in front had been absolutely cleared as a result of the grenades, and the trenches there have been roofed with sandbags. Monty's platoon is down below somewhere, at the bottom of the wadi, between Mike and myself.

We dare not put sandbags round our trenches, as they would only make us more conspicuous. Nor can we dig any deeper, as the ground is too hard; this means that the sergeant and I have to sit with our backs perpetually bent if we are to avoid sticking our heads over the top during daylight.

21st April

Half an hour ago we were in the middle of a bout of rifle grenading. It has taken me some time to gather up my wits and start writing this. Squash's trench looked as if it were the target. Yesterday, at midday, it was Corporal Peter's; then, in the afternoon, Bishop's.

There appears to be just one rifle firing. The man who operates it can be as slow and deliberate as he likes. If his grenade falls twenty feet away from his target, he adjusts his sights and the next time it may be only fifteen feet short, and after that ten, and so on.

We at the receiving end hear the soft report as the rifle is fired. There are a few seconds to wait, then comes the whistle, growing louder, louder, louder. We become all tense and it is impossible to breathe, for at first there is no knowing how far away from our trenches the grenade is going to fall. But after a few more have come over, we soon learn to judge.

One grenade fell nearly at the end of Bishop's trench. Lance-Corporal Ribsdale, who shared it with him, had a splinter through his knee, but could not be moved before nightfall. . . .

It must be an act of Jim Eagle's to be brusque and

67

unsympathetic when we are in the line. Back at B Echelon he was perfectly human, although too prone to practical jokes. When last night I tried to explain our circumstances here, he seemed deliberately to want to misunderstand me. 'Utter bilge. What's the use of war if you don't hit back? Be offensive, man. Use your guts. Use your two-inch mortar.'

The only way to use a two-inch mortar is firing it blind from below ground level, i.e. from the bottom of a trench, which is highly dangerous. Although, because of the rocky ground, Sergeant Denholm and I cannot deepen the trench, we have found that it is possible to widen it, so we intend to do this tonight. We will have to keep the mortar bombs stored in the trench with us; in fact, I already have a crate of them under my feet. Our fate will be doubly sealed if we have a direct hit.

I told Bishop and Corporal Peter to take compass bearings on the report of that rifle. I am doing the same, so that tonight I may be able to pinpoint the firer with the help of maps and air photographs. Then woe betide that Jerry if ever we get the two-inch mortar going. . . .

The sun is hot. My helmet makes me giddy, and I don't wear it often. The sergeant has a tummy upset, and has frequent recourse to our supply of old bully tins, which we have to use if we want to relieve ourselves. Yesterday we ran out of tins, and in order to empty one of them over the side, I lifted my head, minus helmet, above the trench. At once there was a *crack*, and a sniper's bullet stabbed into the bank. It was so close that I could feel the rush of wind on my hair.

Sergeant Denholm is a Catholic. He is for ever telling his beads and looking at gaudy pictures of saints that he keeps in his wallet. He has a very clear brown skin, like certain Parsees'; it is so unblemished and unlined that I cannot shake off a morbid vision of what it would look like if hit by shrapnel or a bullet. We never speak much except when it's time for food, and even then the heat makes us feel little inclined to eat. Brewing up on a tommy-cooker presents so many problems that we'd rather do without.

None of the previous platoons who have occupied this position have bothered to bury their bully and conner tins. As a result the slope of the wadi below us looks like a refuse tip, and provides the Germans with the final clue to our exact whereabouts. The stink gets worse every day, and there is a plague of bluebottles.

We have a field telephone connected to H.Q. and by some curious arrangement you can be transferred to any platoon in any other company. The buzzer went last night, and a sepulchral voice at the other end said:

O thou, whose mighty palace roof doth hang
From jagged trunks—

It was Monty, but Jim Eagle butted in and cut us off. Simon, at H.Q. last night, told me that there had been a noise of hammering and German voices in front of Monty's platoon. His company commander rang him up and asked him what was going on. 'There's enough noise here to please Madame Blavatsky.' 'But really, Monty, what do you think the Jerries are up to?' 'Sounds like a nice game of planchette to me.' The result was that Monty was sent out on patrol to get some more 'precise' information. He returned in due course, in a flurry of egg grenades and none the wiser. The hammering continued, until Monty could bear it no longer and shouted at the top of his voice: '*Ruhe da, wir konnen nicht schlafen!*' And that did the trick. . . .

The ground below our ridge is one of the few places where there is still some fairly long grass. Early this a.m., before light, when the sergeant and I had finished our chores and had sorted out the ammo and food, we decided to conceal some trip flares in this grass. As we were driving in the last stake, the Jerries sent over a Very light. We could only stand stockstill and freeze. The light fell almost at my feet – now there are singe marks on my trousers. I must have been completely illuminated. Yet there was no spandau fire. . . .

To reach Company H.Q. we must climb down a thirty-foot rope into the wadi. Indeed, the rope is the only way of escape from here. As Bishop remarked, on his return from taking Lance-Corporal Ribsdale to the F.A.P.: 'At Steamboat Bill's we were bloody moles. Now we are bloody monkeys.'

Last night Jim Eagle determined to inspect my platoon positions, but he and his runner lost the way and couldn't find the rope. He walked too far along the wadi, until – as it happened – he reached a spot immediately below us. There he was startled to hear stealthy movement in the undergrowth, and he realized in the nick of time that a Jerry patrol was approaching. All he could do was to press himself flat against the side of the wadi, whilst the patrol passed by. There were five Jerries in all, and they blundered straight into Monty's lines. A spirited battle ensued, and I did my best to help out by firing my brens from up on top – with the result that – unknown to us all – Jim was caught between two fires, and both sides' grenades were popping off all round him. No wonder in the end he decided to give us a miss.

I always have qualms when I climb down that rope, in case a Jerry patrol is lurking at the other end. One of our most troublesome feats is lugging up the water-tins without letting them clank against the cliffside.

Later. – I've now managed to fix up my rifle so that I can fire it in the direction of the Jerry lines, without having to put my head above the top. Every so often I loose off – I can't aim, of course, and I don't even shoot at a target. My idea is to make the Jerries think that we, too, have a sniper at work.

Tonight I mean to do the same sort of thing with my brens. At intervals I shall blaze away vaguely towards the enemy, at no specific targets. Keep 'em on their toes, as I'm sure Jim Eagle would say.

Baxter doesn't like being on his own in the adjoining trench. He keeps putting his fat raw-beef face over the side to see how we are getting on – it's just possible for him to do this without being exposed to the Jerries' view. He hardly ever has anything to say to us; all he does is to mutter 'Oh dear; oh, dear,' shake his head, perhaps cluck his tongue once or twice, and then sit down again.

The birds seem strangely indifferent to the general racket. A wren is constantly flitting about in the bush behind us, and nightingales sing both day and night. At dawn we hear the cuckoo.

22nd April

Before dusk last night we were subjected to another very concentrated rifle grenade attack. There was one casualty, Meadowcroft, who caught a piece on his chin. Squash is in a poor state, and had to be held down yesterday morning, when his trench was under fire.

Then came dusk; immediately Mike's platoon, across the valley, became involved in a skirmish with an enemy fighting patrol. Tracer flew wildly in all directions; grenade bursts made silhouettes of the ragged shapes of trees. Then the fighting died down, and there was silence for about ten minutes.

Suddenly more firing, on a much larger scale. It was obvious that the Germans were trying to overrun Mike completely. Tracer again everywhere, grenades in fast succession, with hardly a break between explosions; splatter of brens, schmeissers, tommies; flares, shouts. General alarm, then Action Stations over the telephone. We waited for our turn, listening helplessly to Mike's ordeal.

The buzzer went again. 'Box barrage coming *now*,' Jim Eagle's voice snapped at me. I hadn't heard of a box barrage before. Almost before I'd replaced the receiver, our own heavy mortars' shells were thundering down, closer by far than any accepted danger limit. They hemmed us all round. We were caught beween blazing screens. Then came the artillery, and the din was more monstrous yet. Right and left they fell, in front, behind. The crashing and the roaring swamped the small arms' fire. The hillside rocked and vast flames cracked open the night sky. Sparks and shrapnel hailed on us. It seemed incredible that a shell would not fall short. We were choked by the fumes of cordite. I wanted to shout with laughter.

The barrage continued for a long time – I could not estimate how long. It stopped very unexpectedly, and there was absolute quiet – the quietness of death, and a nightingale sang in the smoky darkness.

But the Germans were not to be crushed. Soon they were sending over more grenades again at Mike's platoon. Then there was a cry, as of the most intense agony, but also of despair and loneliness. It was so shrill and so short, with such an unearthly ring, that I thought it must be some sort of hallucination, an echo of the screaming shells, still whirling in my brain like the inside of a conch. Another cry followed, the same voice and more drawn out; and another, gradually fading into sobs, which became articulate: 'Darling, darling, oh, darling, darling, darling . . .' each word more and more faint until the last was smothered by a further volley of grenades.

From then onwards the whole night was punctuated by these rifle grenades, mingled with the panic bursts of machine-guns. Once we heard German voices arguing. When Mike sounded particularly hard pressed, I would fire my own brens up the valley in the hope of creating some sort of diversion.

Hours passed before the smoke from the box barrage finally cleared; it heaved and writhed below us in grey luminous clouds. A flare set the brambles alight by my trench. Things looked like getting out of hand; the undergrowth was very dry and the flames spread quickly. We had to dash into the bushes and stamp out the flames with our boots – making ourselves easy targets for the spandaus, which – amazingly – spared us.

Towards daybreak there was a big air raid over Anzio, and the sky was riddled with flak.

At last came dawn, but with the prospect of another night and new attacks. . . .

It was during the air raid that Monty telephoned me. 'What *do* you think? A letter from Ursula. A *rat* in the Club Twenty-Nine. Imagine the screams, women jumping on chairs. . . .'

24th April

For the last two days Mike's platoon had been under a constant bombardment by mortars and rifle grenades. Thank God that was not happening six weeks ago when I was there.

We – my platoon, that is – have now been moved and are now in a less exposed area just above Company H.Q., called Fossa della Cogna on the map. Whenever I go down to visit H.Q., which is in the bed of the wadi, I see casualties being carried past. Yesterday evening there was something on a stretcher that was the worst sight I have seen at this beachhead ... *and it was still alive*. Then today there have been seven casualties all from Mike's platoon; six of them had to be carried, and on one of the stretchers, soaked in his blood, I saw Taffy Wright who sailed in the same boat as me from England. What must the effect be on the survivors up there, and particularly on those nineteen-year-old reinforcements, just arrived last week? You can see the strain on everyone's face. Simon looks really ashen, as it is his job to 'control' the casualties when they pass through our lines.

Jim Eagle had a small wound on the shoulder yesterday. He had to be taken back to the F.A.P. in full daylight across the open fields under the Red Cross flag. But he insisted on returning after nightfall. Whilst he was away I was acting second-in-command, with Simon as company commander. This meant having to take over the controlling of casualties for a while. Finally, Simon was called to Battalion Headquarters and I was on my own, in charge of the company. It was then that an enemy smoke bomb dropped very near our H.Q., less than ten feet from an ammo dump. Sparks flew all over the place, and we all shrank back to safety – all, except the C.S.M., who tore out and poured a canful of drinking water over the bomb. Jim says he will recommend him for the M.M. for this.

Simon had been summoned to Battalion H.Q. for a round robin about an episode that took place when an officer was wounded recently. It was Eric Stogumber of A Company, and he had gone out to recce the ground somewhere near Mike. Out in no-man's land he stepped on a shoe-mine and had to be abandoned there by his patrol. I believe he lost a foot. Our stretcher bearers went forward under the Red Cross flag, and so did the Germans. Both parties arrived simultaneously; after exchanging cigarettes, they tossed for who should take away Eric, and the Germans won.

Simon says that he does not believe that the bad cases we see carried by on stretchers feel any pain. He has always heard that severe wounds cause numbness. When I told him about those screams we'd heard from Mike's platoon after the box barrage, Simon said that he thought the man was not crying out through pain, but because he was afraid of dying. Actually, as I have since heard, the man has not died.

Many people regard bravery in small matters – a cut finger for instance – as a question of self-control. This, one comes to realize, is not entirely true. 'Guts' are something you are born with, and a man who is brave over a minor hurt will also be brave when he is dying, or thinks he is dying, with a bullet through the neck. Of course even a courageous man – by which I mean courageous in battle – can in the end be afflicted by bomb-happiness, yet it always turns out that he knows how to control himself when *in extremis*.

But courage – bravery – in battle is a strange thing. It is a question of circumstances very often. Most cornered animals will fight to the death.

I showed Simon a somewhat facetiously cynical letter from a friend, now running a mess in Algiers. In the letter there was a flippant and quite unserious remark about hoping that I was pulling my weight in 'this Great Crusade against the Modern Tamerlane'. Simon flared up immediately. All this talk about crusades made him retch, he said. The Four Freedoms and German 'inhumanity' were quite incidental as issues. Wars were like migrations of insects – a matter of mass impulse, rarely had they anything to do with sentiment; their roots were nearly always buried in much more intricate matters, mainly economic, over which the emotions of the little man, be he German or British, had absolutely no control. . . .

There is very little for us to do in this new platoon area,

75

except to keep out of the way of the heavy stonking. Our dugouts are merely caves scooped from the side of the wadi. Moving about is difficult because of the many loose boulders; we have to rely for support on the overhanging branches of trees. I always seem to be slipping and now both my thumbs are bandaged. As Toumi would undoubtedly say, now at last I look the full seasoned veteran.

All this shelling is the penalty of being farther away from the Jerries. Before we were at least so close as to be below the range of the mortars. Just over the top from here Mepacrine is in another of his lookout posts, again with American spotters. This time I envy his job even less. The Germans are always hurling shells over at the post and there are many hits. Yet it is so solidly constructed that Mepacrine says that only a high explosive bomb from an aircraft would penetrate.

I find it bewildering the way our own and the Jerries' positions are so *interwoven*. There is no hard and fast straight line as the front between us. Moreover, the Jerries still seem to control the main vantage points, and roughly speaking they are dug in round three of the four sides of the battalion area. The men keep on asking why we don't press forward and drive the enemy back – any risk is better than our present conditions. The answer is that there are more wadis beyond, and at the expense of much blood we would only be in exactly the same predicament, but with lengthier lines of communication.

I shall never again be able to listen to nightingales with pleasure. They will always remind me of the Fortress. Little did Keats know how the meaning of his words could be applied:

Fade far away, dissolve, and quite forget
What thou among the leaves hast never known,

The weariness, the fever, and the fret
Here, where men sit and hear each other groan.

Darkling I listen; and for many a time
I have been half in love with easeful Death—

This is Keats country without doubt. Verdurous glooms
and winding mossy ways.

Now more than ever seems it rich to die,
To cease upon the midnight with no pain,
While thou art pouring forth thy soul abroad
In such an ecstasy!

But however much these blasted birds trirrup and
gurgle, they'll never make me feel that it will be rich to die
in the Fossa della Cogna, pain or no pain. Nightingales
are supposed to sing when they are alarmed; the cock bird
is trying to attract intruders away from the nest. Certainly
the noisier things are here, the more they sing. At first we
were entranced to hear them, but now they MADDEN
us. . . .

When the mail came last night, there arrived for me the
long-promised portrait photograph of Jo. She had written
'Love from Peakaboooooo' on the back, which made me
ashamed to show it around. However, the C.S.M.'s
remark, 'Cor, she's a smasher,' gave me confidence, and
now my stock seems to have gone up no end.

26th April

Just now Sergeant Denholm was wounded. A small piece
of shrapnel lodged in his forearm, pinioning his shirt. It
was quite an insignificant affair, but he went so pale that I
thought he would faint. We had been sitting outside our

77

dugout at the time, and the shrapnel passed an inch or two in front of my stomach before it hit him. That's the third near escape from shrapnel since I've been here. *St. Christophe te protège*.

The remarkable Mike has been relieved from the forward platoon. He looked quite unperturbed, and I asked him how he managed to stand up to that rifle grenading. 'Vat 69', was his answer. Which is perfectly true, so I'm told; Mike's runner went bomb-happy, and Mike was seen sitting on the man and taking long swigs from a flask.

Lance-Corporal Ribsdale is back with us, having been patched up after his wound. He said that Bishop talked fishing all through the worst moments up in our last position. What got Ribsdale down particularly, he said, was the way Bishop smacked his lips every time he so much as mentioned the word 'fish'.

My platoon has been given a piat, a curious home-made-looking weapon that I've never come across before. The bombs are like the headless bodies of outsize hornets, and you can send them between seventy and a hundred and twenty yards. The whole principle is based on a tremendously powerful spring. Every time you fire it, however, there is always that small suspicion that something will go wrong and that the bomb will fall short, just slithering out of the end of the muzzle. Yet the contraption fascinates me – it gives such a big bang and causes such a huge cloud of smoke; the Germans must think we have a new secret weapon. I take vicious delight in having my own back on those cold-blooded wretches who were lobbing rifle grenades at us – I can just reach them from here. The piat is a superb morale-destroyer; the blast must be devastating. Simon is amused by my enthusiasm and calls me Piat Trevelyan.

I took two 'prisoners' last night. Lying in my dugout I

heard a faint stealthy rustling in the dead leaves outside. For one horrid moment I thought it was a patrol, then I decided *snakes*. But it was a tortoise. He at once became the platoon mascot, and was christened Tedesco. Then another turned up and so the first was rechristened Ted, and the second was called Esco. According to the (probably incorrect) system of counting the plates on their backs, Ted is seventeen and Esco fifteen. We are going to take them both back to B Echelon. Baxter wants to bore a hole in their shells so that they can be tethered, and he is also intending to polish them up with rifle oil.

Once we are at B Echelon, I mean to shake off Baxter as my batman. He is such an earnest, clumsy, garrulous old thing. Having been what he calls a rural labourer in civilian life, his conversation seems to run entirely on turnips and compost.

The rain has come back, and we are wet and rather miserable.

CICADA VALLEY

9th May

AFTER another brief spell resting at B Echelon, we are back among the wadis. This time we are farther inland at a place called Michele, near the 'Elbow', regarded popularly with even greater awe than is the Fortress. Mine is the forward platoon of the battalion. The landscape is stark and dried up – no bushes, no undergrowth. Days of verdurous gloom are past. We are in pure cicada-land.

There is a lot to write about. First, I am very cross at being in the line at all, since I was promised, after the Fortress duffy, that I should be sent on a three-weeks' intelligence course at Salerno. That would have meant Paestum too – one of my lifelong goals. Adrian, just back from his malaria, has also been on the Salerno course, and he had promised me an intriguing medley of introductions from flighty *duchesse* downwards. Then, all of a sudden, came a complete *volte-face* by the Colonel; my course was cancelled owing to a 'shortage' of officers, and not only this, but I was sent up here to the least enviable sector of the whole battalion front.

I have to admit that so far life at Michele is not nearly so arduous as it was for Mike at the Fortress (that position of his, incidentally, was captured by the Jerries – or Krauts, as it's become fashionable to call them – only three days after our battalion was relieved).[1] The ground being so very open, we are not at such close quarters with the enemy. Their nearest post must be seventy yards off. There is a good deal of mutual stonking, but rifle grenades are definitely *démodés*.

Our present valley is much shallower than that at the Fortress. I imagine we are in an upper reach of the Moletta. In fact, I can see where it peters out, fifty yards from this dugout, at a ruined house we call R.A.P. because of the big red cross painted on it.

R.A.P. is a relic of the days in January when the front line was farther forward. Our blokes were beaten back to here by the Jerries, and there was a real old massacre. The remains of the B——s were cut off at this very spot; the South V——s battered their way through to try to save them, but they in their turn were left with few survivors. All along the bed of our wadi are rough crosses, made of bayonets or sticks, even two rifles tied together, capped by shrapnel-torn tin hats and with identity discs slung over an arm. A new recruit to my platoon says that he was actually with the South V——s at the time. He tells me that Tiger tanks came unopposed right up to R.A.P. and just blasted our trenches.

In many ways this place is the classical setting for a battlefield of the 1917 vintage: shattered farmhouses, bared to their plaster walls, marked with vaccination scars; those crazy imitations of the Christian symbol, over the graves of men who most likely have never heard of Jesus except as a swear-word in American gangster novels; the gnarled trees, white as if some monster hand

---

[1] Many years afterwards I had a letter from someone who visited the Fortress after the Front had moved forward from Anzio. 'On the left flank,' he wrote, 'there was a place where only six paces separated one of our roofed-in two-man weapon pits from the German trenches. Jerry, however, was some five feet higher than us, and used to roll grenades down the slope, trying to get them into our firing slots.'

had peeled them; scrolls of rusted dannert wire; abandoned weapons of all sorts, from primed grenades to anti-tank guns; the brooding dark shapes of burnt-out lorries – all in a wasteland of churned-up earth and craters.

A derelict Tiger stands not far from R.A.P. Perhaps it is one of the ones that caused so much slaughter among the South V——s. Even its silence is a threat. Everything in this valley is too silent.

Son of man, can these bones live? And there was a noise, and behold a shaking, and the bones came together.

In contrast, the houses of Velletri, whose shapes we can now see quite clearly, look daffodil-yellow and alive against the dark woods behind. It was unexpected, the first morning, to find ourselves so close to the Alban Hills. We can even make out the arches of an aqueduct.

We find it a great boon here to be able to wander freely up and down the valley during daylight. Even the most forward bren posts can be reached by crawl trenches. Recently I was helping to extend one of these trenches, hacking away with my pick, when I uncovered a black boot which soon showed itself to contain a human foot protruding from an unmarked grave. A sense of sneaking desecration made me hastily shovel earth over the thing. In so doing I dug up another object, much worse, green and slimy.

All day long we sap up to the rim of the wadi, so that we can bring our brens forward and cover a wider stretch of open ground over the top. We know that Jerry is doing the same. I sometimes wonder if eventually we will meet.

Our sleeping trenches are soundly built. They are all roofed in, and – as at the Cogna – some are entirely hollowed out of the bank, with enough room for two men to lie down in each. I share mine with Sergeant Chesterton, only recently returned from his leave in Naples. He doesn't look a bit refreshed and was in better form when we were at Steamboat Bill's.

Of a morning, when there is time for relaxation and members of the platoon are sunning themselves, visible only to their waists as they lean out of the entrances to their burrows, the scene is like some back alley in the East End, with all the housewives gossiping over the area walls. We only lack the washing hanging out to dry. Baxter was highly tickled when I told him this; little did he realize that he, more than anyone else, reminds me of some red-eyed old nag fresh from the Mile End Road. Bishop, in the next-door trench, obviously thought Baxter was crackers when the latter shouted out to him: 'Morning, Mrs. Bishop. Nice weather we're having today, ain't we? How's your old man's lumbago?'

An air of uneasiness hangs over us – an uneasiness about the general set-up at the Beachhead. There were so many rumours of a push on Rome when we were last at B Echelon. It's not unlikely that the Germans may get windy and decide to mop up some of our outlying posts, of which mine is a perfect victim. We are so isolated here. Even members of Company H.Q. can't reach us by day, and as for the rest of the Battalion – Monty, etc. – goodness knows where they are and whether they could send help if trouble broke out. It's a regular feature of one's existence at the Front that the high-ups should keep us entirely in the dark about what's going on, particularly as regards the disposition of our own troops.

A fine example of the shambles that this can cause was the other night when we arrived at Michele. The Germans had been given warning of the changeover and caught us very neatly up on a ridge at precisely the most awkward moment. We of course hadn't had an inkling that they were so close and had been taking no special precautions. The only cover we had was a mere furrow of a crawl trench, ludicrously inadequate.

For a long time we were pinned down up there in the thick of spandau fire, with tracer flipping at us from every quarter. The night was pitch black, so at least the Jerries couldn't pick us out individually, as they might have done if it had been last night, under the moon; on the other hand, the darkness helped to add to the confusion, and created such a panic among the men as I hadn't come across before. They were mainly afraid that the Jerries would start stonking us.

The real crux of our troubles was that the crawl trench was not wide enough for two bodies to pass one another without exposing themselves to the danger of being hit by a bullet. The men from the unit we were relieving were coming from the opposite direction at the same time, and made no secret of their desperate anxiety to get away as speedily as possible. Their officer kept shrieking at us: 'For heaven's sake, there, get a move on, get a *move* on,' in a high-pitched nasal Public School voice, until somebody from my platoon silenced him by yelling back: 'Shut yer trap, Lah-di-dah.' In our uncertainty and helplessness I could only think of 'Zombie' Davenport's famous maxim at Retford: 'When in doubt, powder heavily.' At one moment we were jammed head to toe, completely immobile, with volleys of tracer like whip lashes a matter of inches over head. It was the complete *All Quiet on the Western Front* film set once more.

Six of my men were wounded. Someone had a bullet through his head and was screaming loudly. No one attempted to help as they passed him. I eased myself up, wondering what on earth to do, when stretcher-bearers arrived. They stumbled over the hillside, waving their flag, but the fools didn't seem to realize that the Germans couldn't see a red cross in the dark – they were only attracting attention by wagging this large shape on the skyline. They were quickly mown down. Then more stretcher-bearers came, and the same thing happened.

Porter was one of my wounded. I don't think he was badly hurt, but he cried out a great deal. When I tried to soothe him, he struck at me wildly, spitting like a jaguar. 'Let me go, you — — fool.' He suddenly sprang up and bolted away into the night. I haven't heard if he survived.

Porter's behaviour quite petrified the other members of his section. Although we had nearly reached the end and were but a few yards from the Michele wadi, they refused to budge. So I had to go back and fetch each one singly. That meant five separate trips.

When light came, I found my hands covered with blood – whether Porter's or from that other fellow who screamed so, I don't know.

10th May

One panicky devil in our forward lookout post last night reported that he had seen Jerries moving round R.A.P. house. I had to pass on this bit of information to Jim

85

Eagle, who at once got het up and ordered me to send a recce patrol up there tonight. He also came to visit me after stand-to – by doing so running some risk, as the ground between ourselves and H.Q. is supposed to be under observation – and averred that he could see two stick grenades lying on the edge of a trench in front of R.A.P. I had a look myself through the glasses, but it was impossible to say whether he was right or not. A trench – well, yes, perhaps – but those 'grenades' could have been anything.

At the prospect of this patrol, universal gloom settled on the platoon. If the Germans indeed occupied R.A.P. by night, then it stood to reason that they would have spandaus sited on every approach; in fact, there was only one conceivable approach we could use, and that was up this wadi without a stick of cover anywhere. We also had to face up to the probability of mines.

After Jim had left, I went on studying the ground through my glasses. A brainwave hit me – why not crawl up there by day? There would be no risk of ambushes and spandaus, and if I went solo I could feel my way inch by inch for mines. On my own I would also be less prone to draw the attention of watchers at Crocus, another ruined house in enemy hands – now little more than a mound of bricks surrounded by a huge nest of concertina wire, and presumed to be held as an observation post by the enemy.

I set out not long before lunchtime. I had my brens covering both Crocus and R.A.P. Everything worked without a hitch. I found that I was out of view from Crocus nearly all the way, as indeed would have been the case if I had walked up there at the stoop. There were no mines, but I did come across a rusty trip-wire; it could have been there for months, so rather than tamper with it, I hauled my body caterpillar-wise over the top.

Jim had been right. In front of the house not only was there a neat little slit-trench, but I also found stick grenades – four of them instead of two. The trench did not look very new, and was without any signs of recent occupation, except that I found a German paratrooper's forage cap at the bottom. All four stick grenades and the forage cap went into my haversack.

The inside of R.A.P. was entirely filled with rubble and therefore uninhabitable. I funked going round to the other side, although I didn't say so to Jim Eagle in my report afterwards. But I did notice something serious: in front of the wire by Crocus there was a number of very considerable earthworks, and they were obviously recent. This leads one to suppose that Crocus is occupied day *and* night by the Germans, and it can't be more than fifty yards from our own lines.

Jim was surprised when I brought back this information so soon. After I'd telephoned, he even braved the danger strip between here and H.Q. so that he could inspect the forage cap at first hand. However, he was sceptical, and mumbled that there was no guarantee about how long it had been lying in the trench. Quite against my most logical instincts, I felt furious with him for this, and I *wanted* a Jerry patrol to be occupying R.A.P. all night and every night. As usual these tendencies to such schoolboy masochism were very swiftly dashed, when Jim said something about 'having to see' whether my platoon ought to keep a standing patrol up there 'to be on the safe side'. Apparently Divisional Headquarters want a prisoner so that they can identify the unit opposite me. Oh, blast, all that over again. . . .

Later. – In the afternoon I went to inspect the new crawl trench that the forward section is extending up over the lip of the wadi. I want to make a proper bren site up there, so that at night we can cover the whole of the area between ourselves and Crocus. In the course of investigations I found a German helmet in the grass. I put it on, and then went down into the wadi and poked my head into Squash's dugout. He was asleep, so I shouted: *'Los, Schweinhund!'* in a fine gruff Teutonic voice. Poor fellow, he looked apoplectic. It was a new experience to be face to face with someone to whom one was the cause of such abject terror and I was ashamed.

Soon afterwards the joke was on me. When I took off the helmet I found that it had been full of dried blood and my hair was thick with the stuff.

I returned to the crawl trench, and found that there was an old shell-hole a few yards in front of it. A slight indentation in the turf ran between, so that you could worm your way across and be up there, observing the enemy lines through field glasses. This I did, and it was not long before I caught sight of a string of helmets and packs bobbing along a ditch, some two hundred yards away. Obviously, a new lot was taking over, so I hurried to give instructions for a plastering by our mortars.

Back to the shell-hole again, in order to observe the shells falling. They were a long time coming, so long that I got bored and took to sweeping the countryside with my glasses, hoping to catch sight of some other titbit I could report on. I was focusing on two hundred yards; it was startling, therefore, when I dropped my glasses and saw with my unaided eyesight a German only a few dozen yards from where I was lying – he was leaning nonchalantly against some gutted vehicle straight ahead of me. My next actions were absolutely mechanical. Without hesitation I raised my rifle, aimed, fired. It was obvious that a bull had been scored by the way he sagged to his knees, then lay in a hunch without moving. It pleased me to have done this, and all the time I was aiming at him, I felt nothing but elation and a pounding excitement. In fact, my sensations were not unlike when I used to stalk roosting pigeons in the elms at the edge of the Hart Wood at home.

There is a cockiness among the men such as never existed at the Fortress. At least we do feel that we have the initiative and that we can now take our turn in being b-minded. Each of my section commanders has a compass, with instructions to take a bearing on the reports of enemy mortars or spandaus immediately they fire, within an approximate range of two hundred yards from here. By drawing pencil-lines from these bearings along a map, we can trace the weapons' exact locations. As at the Fortress, in fact. Then, with great glee, we open up with a piat or two-inch mortar, and by the same system of compass bearings we can tell if the bombs are landing nicely on their right targets.

I have a theory, that in situations like this – like being in Cicada Valley, I mean – it is essential to build up an *esprit de corps*, however bogus, in one's platoon. People must think that the very fact that they are in *my* platoon makes them superior to all the showers in the other platoons of the Company. I have been working on this somewhat Hitlerian theory ever since Steamboat's, and now it honestly does seem to be succeeding. The odd sneer at the other platoons is part of the technique. 'No wonder,' I say when I hear that some unfortunate colleagues have been badly beaten up by an enemy patrol. 'Just what you'd expect from Six Platoon.' Then, to explain away our being sent up here to Cicada Valley: 'Naturally the C.O. has to choose *us* when dirty work comes along. Imagine Six Platoon even trying to cope!' And saying this even helps me to swallow my own resentment at not being sent on that course at Salerno.

It was gratifying at B Echelon to have one or two first-class men applying to join me. The most exciting acquisition was Lance-Corporal 'Lanky' Fields; he has a superb reputation and is one of the few Catania Plainites to have kept a sound nerve. Of course, his china, Macdonnell, had to come with him – even more to the good; I don't care what gossip says about them.

Another new man I am glad to have is a full corporal with the unexpected name of Absalom. I can't at this stage decide quite how reliable he will turn out to be. He always makes a great show of being fearfully keen and neatly turned out. My prep-school motto would have suited him: 'Be Clean, Straight and Keen.'

11th May

At about midnight Corporal Peter whispered to me that he could hear digging to the right of Crocus. Together we edged up to our wire and, sure enough, the blurred shapes of a party of Krauts could be seen flitting about against the star-speckled sky.

We hoiked the piat into position and aimed a bomb at the ground just below them. It was a beautiful shot. I'd never heard a piat explode with such a bang.

At least half a dozen separate voices could be heard sobbing and moaning afterwards. Evidently the other Germans at Crocus were too afraid to fetch back their wounded, as we heard these wretches crying out for at least an hour. I found myself telling Squash in detail about what we'd done, just so that I could see the expression of revulsion on his face.

But those cries haunted us – they went on and on like a reproach. Sergeant Chesterton, in the same trench as me, had to cover his ears.

I could not allow myself to give in. I had to be callous like that. The only remorse that I did feel at the end of it came from the realization that it was so *easy* for me to be callous. Something has happened to me these last days; my mind has silted up. I kill with as much detachment as if I were a robot. Except that a robot wouldn't enjoy killing. . . .

The Colonel paid us a visit in the early hours. He brought with him an unusually taciturn Monty. At the news of their arrival, thin moon-chilled faces loomed like spectres from black holes in the side of the wadi. Monty gave them one look, then scanned the crosses marking the graves below. 'Good Grief,' he muttered, 'what's going on here? Hallowe'en? *Timor mortis conturbat me.*'

The Colonel, on parting, said: 'If you want anything, be sure to let me know.'

Which reminds me, Nanny Matthews has written a letter in answer to one I wrote to her from my trench the first time I was at the Fortress. She says: 'I don't know, dear, how you stand up to all this. You were so carefully brought up.'

Her letter will have to join the family collection in due course, along with the one I wrote, aged 11, to my parents after the Quetta Earthquake: 'Dear Mummy and Daddy, I hear you have had an earthquake. There are two tulips out in my garden. . . .'

12th May

Rumour, not confirmed, says that a major offensive has opened on both the 5th and 8th Army fronts. Certainly our artillery intensified its barrage last night. When we looked at the aqueduct at Velletri first thing this morning, it had been blown in half. Jerry was obviously agitated too, and sent up a constant salvo of flares. To keep the pot a-boiling, I occasionally let him have a few mags from our brens.

At 10 a.m. there was an attack scare and we were given

orders for a hundred per cent stand-to. This in itself was fishy, as neither we nor the Germans attack during daylight unless we really mean very big business. The silence and the suspense, coupled with the lack of news from H.Q., became tedious, so – having already established the principles of the game – I decided to crawl forward on my own and have a dekko at Crocus.

There was a convenient shell-hole not far from the concertina wire on our side of the house. It was the farthest away from our position I'd ever been in this way. However, I saw nothing of particular interest and returned.

Ten or twenty minutes later, back in my dugout, I realized that I had left my field-glasses in that shell-hole. I took my Winchester (the one from Steamboat's), and made my way back there, this time rather less warily. But I couldn't find the glasses, although I spent quite a time searching for them.

During my search I happened to raise my eyes towards Crocus. What I at once saw made me catch my breath. Less than thirty yards off, beyond the wire, a German was sitting behind a spandau.

He had not heard me, and the spandau – looking so much more vicious and purposeful than our homely brens – was pointed in another direction. The man was not wearing a helmet and was basking with evident enjoyment in the sunshine. He was handsome in the classic Teutonic manner, with very blond hair.

As I watched, the German took a comb from his pocket. The sensation of combing his sleek long hair seemed to give him pleasure, as if he were a cat being stroked. Then he yawned, patting his clean hand against his mouth.

I lowered myself into the shell-hole, thinking. It was my duty to kill him, even in cold blood. Again I knew that the thought should revolt me, but again the hunter's urge was too powerful; I aimed deliberately and fired.

But the shot was a misfire. I lay motionless, my face pressed into the dirt. Then, gingerly, I raised myself and looked. The man had not heard and was combing his hair again. Aim at the pupil of his eye, I remembered, and I did, at the pupil of his left eye. Another misfire.

Now I was fearful that I would attract his attention. I therefore decided not to risk another round. Half-way back to our own lines I met Lanky Fields. He had been watching me. 'Take my rifle. Good luck,' he whispered.

There was no option. My intention had been to say nothing at all about the incident to the others. I had to live up to Lanky's misconception of my ability – the misconception that presumably had made him want to transfer to our platoon. This time I stuck dead grass in the netting of my tin hat, so that the strands would help to conceal my face.

Some sound had alarmed the German. He had now put on his helmet and was straining towards me. One hand rested on the butt of his spandau, ready to swivel it round instantly in any direction.

At last this had become a matter of self-preservation. I had to act quickly or he would discover me. I set my sights to zero and fired at him, slap between the eyes.

He gave a little scream – absurdly like the beginning of a hen's squawk when it has laid an egg – and fell backwards.

I was triumphant, again as though after a successful expedition to the Hart Wood – the time when I shot a wild black rabbit, for instance. I hurried back, not bothering much about concealment. Lanky was there to shake me by the hand, and before long I was pouring out the story to an audience, flatteringly impressed.

After the stand-to was over, I was still brimming over with my adventure, so I scrambled over to H.Q. to tell Jim Eagle. But he quickly deflated me. What regiment did the man belong to? Was he a paratrooper? What was the shape of his helmet? All German helmets seem the same shape to me, and I have never learnt to distinguish their regiments. I felt foolish and a braggart, as if the whole thing had been imagined.

Simon followed me from Jim's dugout. 'Well, Killer,' he said, 'so you're in your element at last.' In a flash all my defences had been irretrievably demolished. I could never go there again.

A password had to be fixed for the night. Simon said that we might as well decide on it whilst I was at H.Q. The password is to be Crippen.

13th May

I have been unhappy all night. Oh, God, please let me out of here before I do any more of these things.

We are very tired. There are rumours of Jerry reprisals on us for the attacks in progress round Cassino. Most of the platoon are in a state of jumpy irritability.

Our policy of aggressiveness has to be kept up. Though I cannot face the shell-holes any more, we still have these compass 'precision' barrages with our two-inch mortars, I also have a new toy – a phosphorus grenade. It is made of bakelite, therefore easy to throw. When it explodes, there is a foam of phosphorus sparks which cling to clothing and flesh until they have burnt their way through.

I went to sleep after stand-to, but was awakened by Macdonnell. He had been eating his breakfast when he had happened casually to glance up at a nearby ridge. A German officer and N.C.O. were there, studying the whole layout of our defences with maps and glasses. They popped down at once, but the situation for Macdonnell might easily have become a Crocus in reverse. At least the Jerries can be under no illusions now about our strength in this salient. All of which does nothing to relieve the tension among the men.

I gathered a few grenades, phosphorus and H.E., and went with Macdonnell to just below that ridge. At our approach a swarm of sequin-coloured bluebottles rose up angrily from the bodies of unburied Tommies who we had not known had been lying there – the same bluebottles that we have to be so careful to keep away from the bread ration. We had no time to dawdle and threw a dozen or so grenades over the top. It is impossible to say whether they had any effect, but at least they will serve to show that we intend to stand no nonsense.

14th May

It is nearly dusk and for the first time since I have been at Cicada Valley I really dread the darkness. After that episode of the German officer, an attack can happen any moment and we shall be at a hopeless disadvantage.

I was furious with Lanky and Macdonnell this morning at stand-to. After first light I went on a round of inspection and found them both asleep together under a blanket. That, when they are in the nearest trench to the ridge.

Later in the morning, Sergeant Chesterton – who had been so morose that I knew he was ailing in some way – said to me in the dugout: 'I'm afraid my leave didn't do me any good, sir.' 'What do you mean, Sergeant?' I asked. 'I think I've got a bad dose of clap.' I was inclined to tell him that he'd bloody well have to hang on until tomorrow night, when we are to be relieved. But he was so frightened of letting the disease get a grip on him and he told me that he'd promised his wife that they'd have more children on his return, etc., so I had to decide to let him go back tonight. Corporal Absalom will be acting sergeant.

95

No news from the South. Velletri and Cisterna are being plastered all the time. I wish time could stand still; the present is bad enough, but the fear of the unknown gets us down.

I wonder if this stretch of country will ever recover from its war scars. Coils of barbed wire and burnt-out tanks are, of course, ephemeral objects and will rust away in due course; new houses will appear, and new trees, fully clothed with leaves, will replace these gallows and gibbets so bent in their weary attitudes. Somebody will even attempt to erase the shell-holes, and the bodies will be dug up and carted away to the Allied cemetery at Anzio. So many of the temporary graves here are unmarked, and others have two or three people buried together. Perhaps the War Graves people will arbitrarily give them names of men known to have been killed in this valley – I hope so, for the sake of their families.

15th May

We are sunk in a deep tingling freeze, waiting for tonight. Will the attack come before we can clear out of here? And have the Germans this time been tipped the wink about our changeover? None of us relish the thought of crossing that murderous exposed ridge again, even if safety does lie beyond.

I found a shoot of wild asparagus growing by my dugout today. There are also a few sprays of leucojum in the wadi.

It's unfair that I should have twenty-seven lives so dependent on me.

THE MOLETTA CROSSING

AT last, the true Italy. Heat for my lizard blood, and sky as blue as Ushabtiu. Not a cloud since we left Cicada Valley. I have just returned from a bathe in water that was warmer than ever I knew it round our English coasts.

Well, we had our attack before the changeover. It went off at half-cock, mainly because the Germans didn't send in enough men against us. Probably they only intended a largish-scale fighting patrol. Two hours before our relief was due we had a thorough stonk from their mortars, followed by ten minutes of concentrated tracer fire. The moment this ceased, a score of yelling shapes rushed out of the night, firing schmeissers from the hip. I was with Lanky and Macdonnell in a pit for two brens. Both men were superbly cool. They acted with patent enjoyment, changing mags with streamlined speed.

All our other brens were tearing away along the valley. Some of the Jerry shapes collapsed, others appeared to be driven back into the sky. Then Lanky went mad. 'Take this,' he yelled above the racket, pointing to the butt of his bren and seizing my tommy. He leapt on to the edge of the pit, with the force of a jack-in-a-box. From the corner of my eye I could see him half-bent forward, straining, as though all the virtue in him was being forced into those bullets. A Jerry loomed from the darkness and fell at point-blank range.

Their withdrawal came unexpectedly. There was no shouted command. They must have lost many men, while we suffered only a couple of wounded.

The actual changeover was quiet, and we crossed that ridge without a murmur from the enemy lines. The relieving officer was very raw. It was his first time at the Front, he told me. I took him to Lanky's trench. 'Do you see that black lump over there?' He nodded, frowning. 'It's a dead Jerry N.C.O. We killed him two hours ago.'

I found a fat bunch of mail waiting for me on my return to B Echelon. Toumi tells me that at long last Zombie Davenport has managed to get a base job in Naples. Nobody knows quite what the job is, but Zombie spends most of his time sightseeing in Neapolitan *palazzi*, bribing the maids with cigarettes to let him in through the back door. On one occasion he did this whilst the family was at lunch. Zombie knew that there was a fine collection of Salvator Rosas in the dining-room, so – without saying a word or paying any attention to the people at the table – he walked straight in, clomped round in his army boots, and out again.

Once more we are able to spend much of the day on the beach. Fifteen only are allowed in the water at a time, as it is conceivable that we might be observed by long-range telescopes farther up beyond the Moletta where the shore curves out; there is also the danger of being machine-gunned from the air (though who believes that a Jerry plane would dare venture here in daylight?). Many of the men seem more interested in beetle-racing, on which it is said all their accumulated pay is spent in bets. Any type of beetle can be used, provided it doesn't cheat by flying.

On the spur of the moment, the night before last,

Monty, Adrian, Mepacrine and I decided to have a moonlight bathe. The last time Mepacrine and I had done this was at La Pérouse near Algiers with Toumi, at the cove that Toumi used to call the Sea-witch Cauldron. We were playing the fool and splashing one another, when two anxious tin-hatted little sentries advanced to the edge and pointed sten guns at us. Behind them was a raging R.S.M., who insisted that we should report ourselves to the Colonel. We felt we were losing face badly by giving in, but when we reached the Colonel's tent we found that both he and the Adjutant were having a poker session over a bottle of rum. We were invited to join in. Exit R.S.M., discomfited. The trumpets sound.

Sally still proves a big draw in the evenings. The signals van relays her on a loudspeaker. What a mad nation we are, we British. The Germans can never have dreamt that their programme would be such a success; still less now would they appreciate that it is being a success for the wrong reasons. By way of alternative attractions we have open-air film shows. Last night we saw George Formby.

A great fuss was made about a visit from a Radio comedian – I still can't remember his name. He was to give two informal performances, and we were told to try to persuade as many of our men as possible to attend. The first performance coincided with Sally's hour and was a dead failure; only a handful turned up. Monty and I went to the second, and found that there were only about thirty other people there, mostly officers. 'Like Miss Marty,' Monty whispered to me. 'Miss Marty?' 'Yes. Miss Marty gave a party, and nobody came. Her brother gave another and it was just the same.' We felt sorry for the goldfish-faced 'star'. His jokes were corny, so that we had to pretend to laugh. It was obvious that he was scared at being in the Beachhead; he looked creased – 'Like an old peach, going bad,' said Monty – and kept mopping his forehead.

Some enterprising unit has started its own amateur concert show called *The Beachhead Blues*, which is tremendously popular. Goodness knows how the actors find time to rehearse. One wonders whether they are exempt from front-line service. All the costumes have obviously been filched from evacuated civilians' wardrobes in Anzio. The funniest sketch is about a vamp; on the opening evening the 'girl' was so lusciously made up and padded, and there were such cat-calls from the audience, that Divisional H.Q. had to give orders for her to be made less attractive. . . .

I have paid a visit to Sergeant Chesterton. He has been put in a wired compound, next to the cemetery, with all the other V.D. patients. Mentally, he was in a worse state than ever, and I don't think he welcomed seeing me.

Rumours are strong that Cassino has fallen. We don't like to speculate, but the alternatives for us here are obvious: either we stay put, saving our energies, and wait for the 5th Army to link up, so that we can act as reinforcements for the final drive on Rome; or we immediately break out through the minefields and create some sort of diversion. I believe that politically it will be felt important that we should do something to justify ourselves here, so that people at home won't think that all this time spent at Anzio has been squandered.

Monty and I are planning Victory celebrations in Rome. I have a list of addresses given to me by a friend when I was in York. The names are all wildly improbable, even a Napoleone. My friend gave me strict instructions to eat the list if ever I were captured with it on me.

I bought a sheep from a Rumpelstiltskin living in a house made of bundles of faggots; he is now one of the few remaining shepherds in the Beachhead. The sheep cost me exactly a pound (four hundred *lire*). There were the inevitable sarcastic comments about my motives, but the plan is to hold a Company barbecue the day after tomorrow. Meanwhile, oblivious of its fate, the animal is tethered to the trunk of an umbrella pine near the cookhouse, where it devours most of our cabbage ration. . . .

The time has come for me to look round for new N.C.O.s. Corporal Absalom is still acting sergeant. To my grief, Lanky may have to be transferred to another platoon, as he is to be given a stripe. That will probably mean losing Macdonnell as well.

I wish Bishop would accept a stripe. He refuses because he says it is too dangerous; he wants to see his Romney Marsh and the Royal Military Canal again. I have therefore been driven to force a stripe on Atkinson, a reserved, not startlingly intelligent man, with a sort of constipated look and bushy eyebrows.

We have been joined by a tough little fellow called Manvers, probably Jewish. He combines a boxer's nose and cauliflower ears with wicked elfin eyes and curly black hair. I'd promote him if I knew more of his record. Then there's Toddy Phelan, an Irishman, the platoon clown but a 'rare one' in battle, so they say. All in all, I'm building up a clique of first-class fellows in this platoon, and I mean to stick to them.

20th May. B Echelon

The news is out. Cassino has fallen. . . .

The whole Battalion was called together for an address by some Div. H.Q. brass hat this morning. We squatted in rows in front of his jeep. I think we all felt it was going to be good news – a rumour was going round that the Second Front had started, while Baxter told me that he'd heard there'd been a total surrender by the Germans

on the Gustav line. But we were to be disappointed.
I went with Monty. The brass hat started his har-
angue by telling us how magnificently we – our Battalion
– had been doing; we had suffered casualties but not in
vain; our efforts would be chalked up in the annals of
history. ('*Tiens*, the clichés,' muttered Monty crossly.) As
we were no doubt aware, the Allied troops were doing
frightfully well in the South; that went for the Americans,
the Indians, the Poles as well; we all had to pull together;
never had so many diverse nations shown such team
spirit; the Gustav line was as good as kaput, and soon the
Adolf Hitler line would crumble away.

The brass hat then put on his glasses as if to look at his
notes. This was obviously no more than a reflex action, for
a second or two later they were off again and he was
blandly continuing: the time had come for the troops in
this Beachhead to take action, to break out; there was
going to be a major push in the very near future by the
American armour ('Glory be, not *us*,' whispered Monty);
but Jerry must be kept guessing; there must be a diver-
sionary attack, and this would come from the British
sector. It has been decided that our Division would have
the honour of being the first to break out of the Anzio
Beachhead. (A groan from Monty. 'Stop him, for God's
sake. I don't want to hear any more.') It had also been
decided that our Battalion should represent the Division,
and that we should constitute the first wave of the
offensive.

There was an uneasy stirring among the audience. Although none of us uttered a word, the air seemed to
vibrate with unspoken thoughts, drowning whatever else
he had to tell us. It was as if we had suddenly become
preoccupied by personal problems – a letter from home
unanswered, kit to be sorted out, and the lack of time in
which to do these things. As we drifted away singly,

Simon called to me and said that Jim Eagle wanted all Company officers to report to H.Q. at once.

My forebodings on my way to Jim's reminded me of a rowing race, when you are bent forward with your oar above the water and feel already out of breath and dry-mouthed. Then, when he spoke, I imagined that he was like a coach shouting pep words from the bank. There was nothing that he had to tell us that I didn't already know; it was all inevitable somehow: the Commanding Officer had decided that A Company – ours – should lead the attack. Two of our platoons are to be forward, one in reserve. Mine is to be a forward platoon.

We have been issued with air photographs and maps. The attack is to be across the Moletta's mouth – in fact, along the sand-dunes and the neighbouring scrub. The eventual Battalion objective is a group of bathing-huts called Americano, about three-quarters of a mile beyond the river. You can see the Jerry trenches and the paths joining them quite distinctly on the photographs. My platoon is to be on the left, the side nearest to the sea.

This evening I am to go on a recce patrol along the river, which serves as a boundary between our lines and the Jerries', although there are minefields on either side. Jim Eagle is coming too, so are some sappers. I am to bring my three lance-corporals – Atkinson, Banner and Wyllis-Jones.

Already we have been starting rehearsals. I never thought I would put my O.C.T.U. field drill into practice. We shall first have to charge for about a hundred and fifty yards with fixed bayonets through the Jerry minefield, previously 'softened up' by our artillery. Once we reach the scrub, the platoon will divide into its three sections. I will take the left-hand one, and will head for the Jerry trench that appears most clearly defined on the photographs. . . .

Monty had been tiresome about this attack. He keeps saying that he knows he won't survive it. He wants me to promise to write to Ursula afterwards. I'm afraid that I had to be harsh with him.

He also keeps asking: 'Raleigh, what do you *really* think of me?' The inference being that, if he is killed, do I think that he will have led a worthwhile existence? Simon was with us once when Monty asked me this, and later ticked me off for being so hard-boiled. He said that Monty is a great deal more highly strung than I perhaps realize.

I respect Simon. Everyone has his own, quite individual opinion of another person's character; generally you – the other person – are aware that this opinion is hopelessly wrong, yet you have to play up to it. Monty is like this where I'm concerned, but not so Simon, who sees through me as though I were a window-pane. The other day they were discussing some abstruse point of ethics, when Monty wheeled irritably on me, saying: 'What's *your* view? Damn you, you sit there like a lama, and I never know what you think.' At which Simon said something under his breath about silence not necessarily meaning wisdom. Monty didn't hear, but Simon was of course perfectly right – the truth was that my poor old brain was still miles behind in their argument.

21st May. B Echelon

Last night, the night of our patrol along the Moletta, was also the occasion of the killing and eating of my sheep. There was none of the barbecue spirit I'd planned, and, anyhow, the meat was stringy and tasted of shoelaces. We ought to have let it hang, but there was no time.

As the moment approached for us to leave, I found myself becoming buoyant and talkative. I had smeared my face with black boot polish, and was wearing gym shoes and Aunt Eilie's cap comforter. A jack-knife from the Casa di Cantoniera was stuck in my webbing belt. I couldn't resist showing myself to the Mess, my spirits as usual being dashed by Simon's characteristically tolerant expression.

We drove in two jeeps to that Martello tower behind Stonk Corner. Here we dismounted and were joined by a sapper officer and corporal. The latter was a horny old sweat, but the officer was about my age. There were few heavy guns firing. The whole night seemed to be waiting.

We moved forward on foot through the lines of the S——es, who were holding that part of the Divisional sector. We stopped to report at their underground H.Q. to look at more maps by paraffin lamps.

We passed in single file along an unmarked 'secret' track through our minefield and into the Moletta via a depression where no doubt cattle used to go to drink. The banks farther down were steep, about fifteen to twenty feet high on the average. We waded along the river for at least a hundred yards in this no-man's land. I thought we were going unnecessarily far; anyone could lob grenades down on us, and before long we would be running into the outposts of the Jerries in the wood opposite Steamboat's. However, at last Jim was satisfied, and we returned, having noted such things as the variations in the height of the banks, the potholes in the river, and the existence of a strand of barbed wire, probably an agricultural fence, along the top of the bank on the enemy side.

When we had returned to the depression, there was an argument between Jim and the sapper corporal about the correct way home. This argument seemed stupid to me. I was quite sure of the route we had come by and offered to lead the way. We again went in single file, with Jim Eagle second and the sapper officer third.

I had hardly taken twenty steps when everything went up in a dazzling green flame, and I was numbed by a fierce stab on the nape of my neck. My ears were hammering, and I had the impression that Jim was lifted bodily over me and thrown into a bush. I was down on my hands and knees, half-blinded and dazed, for some moments.

I turned and saw a man lying very still, and beyond him there was another, making soft quick moans. The sapper corporal and I lifted the first. It was the sapper officer. His face looked mostly blown away. He was dead, there was no doubt.

I lifted the other, who was no longer uttering any sound. This was Lance-Corporal Atkinson. The whole of the lower half of his body was gone. I had his head in my hands, and he gave a little gurgle from right inside, and I knew he had died too.

Oh, the smell of that hot blood, and the smell of cordite – Lance-Corporal Atkinson, whom I'd only just promoted.

I must have walked right over that mine. I swear I was leading them along the proper track.

Jim was not really hurt, just stunned. He was vague and helpless. Only the sapper corporal knew what to do next. He took the lead and prodded the way back inch by inch with his bayonet. We all had to hold on to one another's belts. Both Jim and I were very sick when we reached the S—— H.Q.

The sapper corporal never spoke again after we'd reached safety. From the way he looked I knew that he considered I was to blame.

Today I feel better, but when I got back to B Echelon after that patrol I had made up my mind that I couldn't face the 23rd.

Oh, God, please don't let me disgrace myself. I want

Mother so much. I have never needed her like this. Monty and Simon are both on recce patrols tonight. . . .

Lanky is definitely being transferred to 7 Platoon, but not Macdonnell. I am to be given two sappers to carry a Bangalore torpedo in case of difficulties with wire during the attack.

They say that our troops of the 5th Army are only twenty miles away.

22nd May. B Echelon

God give me strength for tomorrow, for I can think of nothing else.

25th May. C.C.S. (Casualty Clearing Station), Anzio

I am here with some grenade wounds. Monty killed, and many others. I can't write more. We are no longer a Beachhead.

27th May. C.C.S.

I am to be sent to hospital in Naples, to have a piece of grenade out of my cheek.

29th May. 186th General Hospital, Naples

. . . We were to attack an hour before dawn. The main American advance towards Cisterna would be going through on our right some while later. My Company was the first to have to cross the Moletta; after we had secured the outlying German trenches, we were to be followed by C, with Monty and Mike, who were to press on to Americano, the final Battalion objective. With a phenomenal artillery and mortar programme laid on, naval diversions up by Ostia, and tanks in support, it ought – we were constantly being told – to be a 'piece of duff'. The sappers were to put up ladders for us on the banks of the Moletta, and the shells were calculated to blast away the wire and set off any mines, besides keeping down the Germans' heads.

I admit now that I was seriously shaken after that recce patrol. I had even thought of going to see the Colonel. The M.O. kept giving me dope, which helped a good deal. Finally I was shamed into pulling myself together by the attitude of the men, who were so cheerful. . . .

After the march up to the S—— positions, we waited in slit trenches until zero minus three-quarters. I even dozed a little. 'Fall in,' and the rehearsal became the real thing. I swallowed a Benzedrine.

The Company trooped off along the white tapes guiding us through our own minefield. All the while immense explosions ripped up the enemy lines. An ammunition dump was hit and we saw great billowing flames of scarlet and orange. It was like walking into a roaring furnace. None of us spoke. We could hear no sound of answering fire from the other side.

Half-way across the minefield word was passed up to me that Squash had shot himself. Time was already short, so we could not wait to unhitch the 38 set that he had been carrying. That meant that my platoon would have no wireless during the attack.

When we reached the river, we found the bodies of sappers lying in the water with their ladders beside them. It was the first indication that our plans would have to be altered. . . . The banks were easier to scale than we'd expected. It was zero minus five by the time the point section had reached the wire fence, where more tapes should have been laid to show that the mines had been cleared.

'But, sir, we can't go through here. Where are the tapes?'

(Zero minus one.)

'Nonsense,' I said. 'Of course there are no tapes. Come on, let's get going.' And I had to crawl out ahead, to show that they'd nothing to fear.

The section lay down on either side of me. Then Absalom with another section came up alongside. There was now the hundred and fifty yards' advance across the open.

'Fix bayonets. Cock your tommy-guns. Have your grenades ready.'

Away at a steady pace – no opposition. Before us the barrage lifted and receded into the bushes. A mine in 7 Platoon's area. Still no opposition. Another mine. One of our men probably this time. Fifty yards to go and . . . 'Charge!' All the old slogging on the barrack square was justified. Someone gave a bloodcurdling yell and we all took it up. I found myself singing aloud.

Jerry trenches gouged out and empty. Fragments of twisted branches. A paratroop helmet.

'Right, Corporal Peter, we'll go down this track. Corporal Absalom, you go round the other side.'

We skirted the outside edge of the bushes. In the half-light and with the deep shadow of the tamarisks, we never saw the spandau until we were right on top of it. It opened up five yards away, a yellow tongue, but gone before I'd realized what had happened. Corporal Peter fell. 'I've been hit, sir.' He said it so calmly that I couldn't believe he was serious or that I, the nearest to the spandau, should have escaped. The man next to him, young Langdon, was whimpering like a puppy, and beyond there were others lying in sprawled attitudes. Remembering my tommy-gun I tried to fire at the bushes. It was clogged with sand, so I threw a grenade and crouched until it exploded. As I ran off, I shouted to Corporal Peter and the rest to make their way back as best they could. But the corporal never answered.

My head throbbed. I was at fault, I suppose, for leading them outside those bushes and across the obvious line of fire. My only thought was revenge. A man lay face downwards, dead. It was Carruthers. I took his tommy-gun. Some members of the reserve section came up and together we tried to work our way to a spot behind the spandau.

The artillery barrage was very close and the shells were falling with a retching crash in the trees and scrub only a few hundred yards farther on. Clods of sand, scraps of branches, and white-hot shrapnel hurtled above us. Some-one said that Absalom had been hit in the eye. Two Germans, silent and grey, came up with their hands above their heads. One of our men ran over them quickly for weapons and appropriated their watches. A helmet dodged round a bush. We chased after it. A shout. 'Look out, behind you!' We threw ourselves face down, the sand spurting over us from a grenade. A jab in my wrist and a taste of blood. I knew I'd been hit, but the pain was slight. Another man had been seriously hurt in the groin, it seemed. We found Absalom sitting on the ground both hands clutched to his eye. My third corporal was nowhere in sight. 'Down, grenade!' It was too late and I felt a stinging slash in my cheek, my left elbow and my knee.

A furious reckless excitement drove us on. At last Macdonnell and I reached the Jerry spandau. Macdonnell threw a grenade. After the explosion I ran to the edge of the dugout with my tommy-gun. There was still a German in it. I tried to use the tommy, but it was jammed again. The German threw a grenade at my face, hitting me on the cheekbone. I felt giddy, but could just see that the grenade had fallen back into the trench. I shouted to

Macdonnell and we dashed back to cover. A spout of earth and sand flew upwards.

The German had gone when we came back again – evidently he'd scrambled to safety down a crawl trench. We pulled out the spandau and rolled it on the ground, to clog up the workings.

There was also a Jerry rifle in the dugout. I tested it by firing in the air, and gathered handfuls of rounds, which I pocketed. It was useless to keep that tommy. Several minutes followed of a crazy hide-and-seek among the bushes. I found Manvers with the piat and he got some splendid shots into what appeared to be a platoon headquarters. The time had come to move forward and I collected as many men as I could. A couple more prisoners, and on we went. I sent all the captured Jerries back with Baxter; I felt he deserved it.

We came to a clearing. At the far end a sand-bagged shack had been built out of shutters and doors. I recognized this as our platoon objective. The place seemed quiet and deserted. Suddenly I felt very tired. Next to me was the Company runner, who had been attached to my platoon for this attack. He was a gentle little man, with a face prematurely old and wizened. His flapping ears reminded me of Dopey. He nudged me and offered a cigarette. We lit up, forgetting that we were standing in the open outside our ultimate objective.

The shack hadn't been made for defence. There was only a small window and the entrance was closed. We advanced gingerly towards it, threw open the door and shouted with a great show of bravado. Silence. We waited indecisively. Ought we to go inside and risk a burst of schmeisser? Perhaps we should throw a grenade? The answer was settled by a figure appearing in the doorway. He was tall and bare-headed, a well-built man with straight, fair hair. He walked towards us, apparently quite composed, without even lifting his hands. The situation was ridiculous. We stood there as he approached, feeling like children in our nervous excited state, guilty children who have been caught with cigarettes in their mouths. Bishop was standing with us. It was he who made the first move.

'Come on, up with those hands,' he shouted.

The German obeyed, a smile twisting upwards for the moment. Bishop ran forward with Dopey and myself, each of us anxious to be the first for loot. Bishop snatched his field glasses, Dopey caught his wrist for a watch, and I searched his pockets. All I found was a large pair of scissors, such as a surgeon might use for cutting away bandages.

Dopey said: 'Blast him, he hasn't even got a watch.'

The German remained silent and aloof, smiling again.

'A flaming warrant officer,' hissed Bishop.

I'd now to decide what should be done with him. I'd only eight men left, and it would be dangerous to send one back as an escort; obviously there were still several Germans about. I gave orders to form a four-cornered hedgehog round the shed.

'He'll have to find his own way back to Company H.Q.,' I told Bishop. 'Just run over him again to see if he's got any weapons, and send him back.'

The German warrant officer submitted to a further search; then, without a word from us he set off to our lines alone.

'Well, that's something cool,' said Dopey. 'He must have understood us all along.'

I took stock of our weapons. We had only about a dozen grenades left between us, four bren magazines, and six tommy magazines. I knew from the air photographs we'd studied at B Echelon that there must be another spandau post to be cleared between the Moletta and ourselves. I told Macdonnell to follow me down a track towards the fringe of bushes that overlooked the sea.

'Our usual game, I should think,' I said to him. 'Chuck a grenade, then in with the bayonet.'

It was not long before we found the position.

'Got your grenade ready?'

Macdonnell nodded. 'You'd better take my tommy,' he said. 'A bayonet and a Jerry rifle won't be much use.'

We crouched low. 'Right,' I whispered.

Macdonnell threw the grenade. We waited, counted the seconds. Nothing happened.

'Damn,' he said. 'I must have forgotten to take out the pin and that's my last.'

All that was left to do was to run up, there and then, and spray them with the tommy.

Two very small and terrified Germans were huddled in the trench. Once more my tommy was choked with sand; it was the third time that morning. One of the Germans fired wildly up at me with his rifle, at a range of about six feet. I felt the scorch on my shoulder.

'Quick,' I said to Macdonnell. 'I've been hit. Tommy's jammed.'

We looked round. A German came out with his rifle pointed at us, and we bolted back among the bushes to our hedgehog.

'All right, let me get that beggar,' said Macdonnell.

He threw himself down by a bren that had been covering us, and opened up as the German appeared round the corner. It looked as if we'd got him, and he staggered back out of sight.

That meant another bren magazine gone. If we didn't get more ammo soon, we would be in serious danger.

'Bishop,' I said. 'You'd better report to Company H.Q. that we've taken our final objective. Tell them that I've only eight men left, counting you, and we're dangerously short of ammo. Tell them about the Jerry post being still occupied. I think it's a case for the tanks. Come back as soon as you can.'

I hated to see him go. Since Steamboat's we had felt a special understanding. I only sent him because he was reliable.

Manvers said: 'There's another Jerry crawl trench along here, sir. Can I finish them off with the piat? We've still got two bombs.'

We came to a pile of sand, camouflaged with branches of tamarisk. Manvers aimed carefully. It was the closest range that I'd ever seen a piat used.

'That'll finish 'em off all right,' said Manvers, as a huge geyser leapt up with a shattering roar.

We found the place quite empty. Manvers was bitterly disappointed.

'What, no bods?' he said.

We returned to our shack and waited for Bishop's return with news from H.Q. My wounds were beginning to throb. I went out and was sick in the bushes.

Suddenly I saw a figure crawling towards us, waving feebly with one hand. Its face was pewter-coloured. I stared, then realized it was Bishop.

'Water,' he croaked.

'My God,' said Dopey. 'He's lost a leg.'

We bent over him. Dopey gave him a drink and removed his helmet. Bishop's leg had been blown off just below the knee. . . . There seemed to be no blood, although his bone was exposed.

He was trying to move his lips. I bent down and heard: 'Jerries still there. Spandau. Had to warn you—'

Then he spoke again. 'Snipers too. Fired three times as I crawled here—'

'Dirty bastards,' muttered Dopey.

We carried him back to safety. Dopey tried to bind up

his stump with a field dressing. . . . I gave him a shot of morphia in the wrist.

'There's a Jerry stretcher here,' said Dopey. 'We *must* get him back.'

Bishop seemed fully conscious. His eyes were wide and glaring, white showing all round the pupils.

'We can't send any more men back,' I said. 'We're short enough as it is. What if there's a counter-attack?'

As we were talking, two more Germans appeared with their hands up. They were very scared.

'We'll get these Jerries to take him back,' I said.

It was the only solution. Bishop, by this time past speech, shook his head angrily. When we found that the canvas of the stretcher was rotten, we made the Germans clasp wrists to form a chair. Bishop fainted as we lifted him.

I still had to send word back to Company H.Q. Manvers volunteered to go.

'No Jerry would ever catch me,' he laughed. 'I'll run all the way.'

He left, and there were now only seven of us in the position.

We never saw Manvers again.

Shortly afterwards, a line of our own men came through the scrub towards us with fixed bayonets. It was Mike's platoon. Mike was in great form.

'For God's sake, Mike,' I said, 'give me some tommy mags and some grenades. I've run out.'

'My dear boy,' drawled Mike. 'Just think of all the men in grey ahead of me. How can I possibly give you any? But for old time's sake, here's one mag and a grenade. Oh, you might as well have our wireless. We dropped it and something keeps tinkling inside.'

He lifted his tin hat. 'Pleasant dreams.' And they disappeared.

Then the tanks came through, creaking and grinding through the tamarisks. We waved at them as they passed, but they didn't seem to notice.

Finally when a messenger came from Company H.Q., bringing news of reinforcements, it really did seem as if the worst was over for us. It was then that I heard that Manvers had never turned up; the messenger said that Bishop had told Jim Eagle where we were. I looked at my watch. It was eight o'clock.

Macdonnell and I went back to that trench where I'd been nearly hit in the shoulder. This time it was empty. Farther down, where the scrub met the mouth of the Moletta, Macdonnell pointed at a patch of grass.

'Good Lord, look at that.'

The grass was glistening with new blood, and in the middle was a pair of field glasses, the same that Bishop had taken from the German warrant officer.

'That's where the poor devil must have copped it.'

'We'd better take those glasses,' said Macdonnell. 'Always useful.'

To our right was the sea, fresh and sparkling. It was odd looking across the Moletta from the enemy side at the quiet bushes from which only recently we'd been peering at this very spot. A few yards up the opposite bank a dead German was lying; he'd obviously been there for months, for he was now almost a skeleton. Farther up the river we could see that the sappers had made a wide plank bridge. They were already carrying across the stretcher cases. Soon I was to be one of them. . . .

30th May. 186th Gen. Hospital

Lights out before I could finish last night. . . .

News came through that C Company – presumably Monty or Mike – had taken Americano. The re-

116

inforcements and some cases of ammo arrived. We were told to dig in, for air spotters had reported a possible counter-attack.

Another German turned up. He seemed to be weeping and held a hand to his eye. He was among us before I had realized he was so close. When he took away his hand, I found that his eyeball was half out of its socket.

'We really ought to help this wretch before sending him on to H.Q.,' I said to Dopey.

We had used up our field dressings on Bishop and on my knee and elbow. Inside the shed we found some Jerry lint, so we tore a strip off the man's shirt and bandaged his face. Then we searched his pockets, and sent him back alone to Company H.Q.

Inside the shed it was very dark, and there was that bitter unwashed-hair smell, so characteristic of Germans in the line; I had noticed it on the prisoners we took at the Fortress. Dopey sat down on a box and tried to make Mike's wireless work.

'Not a sausage,' he said after a bit. 'Completely phut.'

I rummaged around. 'No use looking for loot,' Dopey remarked without looking up. 'We've been through it pretty thoroughly already. Only some Tedeschi A. L. 63, a few postcards of Rome and some bottles of fizzy stuff like champagne.'

I looked at the postcards and the well-known images of St. Peter's, the Colosseum, and Romulus and Remus. I realized how close we were to seeing all these. The Germans, who had inhabited this place, must have gone back to Rome to rest just as we used to go to B Echelon. There were two bunks in the shed, one above the other, and an iron stove. I sat down on the lower bunk, until Dopey reminded me of lice.

The German heavy artillery started up. We heard the

117

shells whining over our heads, and exploding out to sea. We knew that they couldn't be dropping far off, as the sand quaked every time they came down. There was a shout of alarm outside. 'Smoke!' Did this mean the counter-attack? The fumes caught us in the chest. We were spluttering and choking. One shell landed in a clump of dry gorse-like bushes. In a few seconds they were alight. It looked as if the shed would be engulfed. Dopey, Macdonnell and I dashed into the bushes and frenziedly stamped it out. I thought we were like Shadrach, Meshach and Abednego.

Our trousers and gaiters were badly singed, and our faces were coated with soot and congealed blood. The smoke died away and with it our fears – temporarily – of a counter-attack. It then struck me that there was still one part of our area that we had not explored. I hobbled down a path and discovered two Germans cringing under a big tamarisk. They had been sitting there, only a few yards from us, all the time. Something prompted me not to shoot, and instead I put on my most regimental sergeant-major voice and told them to come out, sharp. They obeyed meekly; one man began to sob, but without tears.

They, too, were sent back to H.Q. without escort.

Back to the shed, where Dopey and I sat in silence, cleaning sand out of our weapons and listening to the shells exploding in the sea. The time was two o'clock. The piece of grenade in my elbow sent shooting pains up my veins, and Dopey said that the wound on my face looked swollen and was full of dirt. After I had been sick again, we decided that I should go back to H.Q. and have my wounds dressed, and then return. Dopey would be left in charge.

I stuffed some of the champagne into my pockets, and left.

On the way to H.Q. I passed another shed where I had

thrown a grenade earlier in the day. Two of our men were lying at the entrance, the flies already swarming about their faces. I had to look and could recognize one as Toddy Phelan, the Irishman.

Company H.Q. was in a narrow crumbling sandpit. The shells were falling close and I felt that it had been safer in our warrant officer's shed. Jim and Simon seemed strained, and looked startled to see me – perhaps because of my blood-marked denims. They said that we'd had more casualties than they had expected. They had no first-aid kit and I must go to Battalion H.Q. across the river. Mike had just gone across; he had been wounded in both feet.

Their subdued manner had the effect of making me feel gay, and I began to chatter inanely. I offered Simon some champagne, but he said that it was only a type of Vichy water.

German heavy machine-guns had been mounted in the wood opposite Steamboat Bill's and were covering the Moletta. Jim said I ought to go across on a stretcher under the Red Cross flag. I felt a fraud doing this. 'If you can come back,' said Jim, standing over me, 'please do, as soon as you can. We expect the counter-attack any moment.'

I crossed the river without a shot being fired. Mike was on the other side; he had had his feet dressed and was going back. He looked terribly pale and didn't speak to me.

They insisted that I should be strapped on to a stretcher at the back of a jeep. As they were doing this I saw a spindly major with long moustaches dodging warily from bush to bush, flinging himself down periodically with great flurries of sand. All the time he was quite out of view from the enemy. 'Bomb-happy,' a stretcher-bearer said. 'Quite nuts.'

At Battalion H.Q. I met Adrian, who was Intelligence Officer. He said I must see the Colonel, and then told me that Monty had been killed leading a section in a charge across the open to Americano; all the section had been wiped out to a man. . . .

The Colonel was kind, but I knew that there was little news for me to tell. Someone said that Squash was in a nearby dugout; he had only shot himself through the foot, not seriously. He had sat there crying all day. If I went to see him, it might help. But I couldn't face him.

In the dressing station they gave me morphia before I had time to object. There was a signals officer in there. He came and squatted above me. I recognized him as Mr. Richards, my favourite prep school master. As I went under, he said: 'Hello, Trevelyan. Any better at your Logs since I last saw you?'

PART TWO

Campania

CELIA

30th May. 186th General Hospital

I HAD always thought that the stories about stealing
from wounded men were nothing but Army malice, but
these were the things that were taken off me whilst under
morphia between the Regimental Aid Post and the
C.C.S.: a wrist-watch, a silver flask that belonged once to
my grandfather, a hurricane-proof lighter carried by our
Rector during the last war in Palestine, and my wallet.

I spent four nights at the C.C.S. A Tank Corps subaltern was in the next bed to me. He had been in one of
those tanks that had passed through my platoon position
at the Moletta Crossing, and had actually seen
Monty die. I didn't want to hear the details, but he was
such a brash young man that I knew it was hopeless to try
to convey to him that Monty was a particular friend of
mine. He was the type who considers all war to be nothing
but a jolly game; you die or survive according to the luck
of the draw, and if you die – well, then, too bad and
nobody's going to waste time blubbing about you.

Simon came to see me twice. He told me that the
Germans had put in the counter-attack, and that our Battalion had been forced back across the Moletta. My platoon had been completely overrun; most of the men I had
left in it are still missing. The total number of Germans
sent in against us during the counter-attack was thought
to be six hundred. Simon put our own casualties at two

hundred and thirty, with fifty killed and seventy missing. Towards nightfall, he said, the Germans withdrew again, presumably when they found out that the real Allied onslaught was against Cisterna. I asked him about Monty, and he said that the Padre had made a special journey across the river to recover the body, before it had in fact been confirmed that the Germans had pulled out.

It is rumoured that Monty is being put in for a posthumous V.C. I don't know the full story of what he did even now. Apparently he found Mike's platoon pinned down by spandaus and anti-tank guns only sixty yards from Americano. Although his own men were reduced by casualties to section strength, he rallied them into following him in a great death-or-glory charge across the open. All the while he was cracking his usual absurd jokes and chanting the tune of the regimental march. Every one of them was killed.

I had Ursula on my conscience, but Simon has her address and promised me that he would write to her.

My wounds are not serious. Only my cheek hurts a little; an X-ray has shown that a piece of grenade is sitting there, an inch below the bone. Because of this I have been shipped to the 186th to be operated on by the specialist, the maxillary facial surgeon – known, needless to say, as Max Factor.

There are two other pieces of shrapnel inside me, near my left elbow and below my left knee, but I was told at the C.C.S. that they were not worth removing. If they don't eventually work out by themselves, they will act as useful barometers.

I was taken to Naples in an American Red Cross boat, and shared a cabin with three leg amputation cases. Strangely enough, one of my companions was Bishop. Although he was little inclined to conversation, his face had such an unexpectedly healthy colour that it made me realize that, apart from the shock, the loss of a limb does not affect the rest of one's system as seriously as might be imagined. Certainly the American male nurses seemed to share this point of view, when helping another of the amputation cases, Sergeant Lane, into his bunk. The sergeant was fuming, since he had had his leg off near the hip. 'And yet they flipping well asked me to hop down the corridor.'

During the first advance from the Moletta, Sergeant Lane had been in command of the platoon parallel with mine. He had stepped on a mine within the first five minutes. I remembered hearing the explosion.

The fourth member of the cabin was Chagford, who had also been in my platoon. We had always considered him a bit of a fuss-pot, but at the attack he had really shone. I had seen him throwing out grenades to the right and left like the Sower of the parable in a Biblical oleograph. He had stayed on with Dopey and the rest after I'd left, but managed to escape during the counter-attack. He had been blown up by one of our mines and had had to be picked up by a tank whilst under spandau fire.

Come to think of it, the quiet unspectacular members of the platoon turned out best when finally put to the test – Bishop, Chagford, Dopey, Macdonnell. The flamboyant ones, always boasting and out to impress, invariably let us down. Corporal Absalom, for instance. I now hear that the worst he suffered was a black eye – and he had to leave us just for that.

At Naples docks we were met by some women from our own Red Cross. They plied us with doughnuts, although we'd just had breakfast. Among them was Kitty Sandown, a local from Essex. . . .

This is a 'heads-and-tails' hospital – head wounds and V.D., a droll combination. I fancy the building was once a barracks; it's dingy enough to have been that.

There are a number of stables, and some of the wards look as if they had been storerooms, perhaps for mules' fodder.

I am not confined to my bed, so I can walk about the hospital and sit in the Library if I like. This afternoon I am to have my operation, but in two days' time they say I'll be allowed out in Naples. Soon after I arrived here I started making inquiries about whether there were any fellows from the Battalion also in the hospital. This was uphill work, as no patient appears to be 'documented' until he's been in for some time. At last I found a list with Manvers' name on it, but without mention of his ward. A nice English-speaking Italian, who works as an orderly, suggested that I should try the Clearance Ward, where the bad cases from the 'new intake' are brought before being sent to other wards when vacant beds are available. The last I had seen or heard of Manvers was when I dispatched him as a runner to Company H.Q. during the attack.

The morning was very hot and the sun in the courtyard was enough to make you wish you were wearing dark glasses. By contrast the light in the Clearance Ward was so dim that I had to hesitate in order to accustom myself. All the windows were shuttered, and over the doorway a gauze net had been hung to keep out the flies.

The air inside the ward was loaded with the thick putrescent stench that I had come to associate with very severe wounds. At first I was confused by the Babel of groans and delirious mutterings, the heavy gasping breathing, and the sounds that for all the world might have been bitterns booming on a spring evening. I became aware of two blurred lines of white beds, perhaps fifty in all, and in the nearest I saw grotesque figures, heads swathed like giant mummies'. Some of these kept turning and hitting out clumsily; others lay still in ashy silence as though their souls had already forced an exit through those black circular mouths.

Then I sensed that I was being watched. A Queen Alexandra sister was standing with arms folded by a scrubbed wooden table. I thought how young she looked, and as I went up to her, I was struck very forcibly by the fact that in this great room, packed with so many people, only she and I were in control of our senses and *alive*. But she was also very much more than that – she was in command. I was amazed at her calmness and self-confidence, and at the dignity of her almost patrician features, which at the same time had a remote, unearthly compassion about them. What was more, she was the only member of the hospital staff not too busy to answer questions.

She spoke oddly fast, too fast, without altering the cool tone of her voice, so that I wondered if secretly below this mask of perfect control she was very tired. She told me that the names of the patients were written at the end of each bed; I could walk round if I liked. I started to do this, past bottles of blood plasma dripping into cinder-coloured bodies, past enamel buckets full of dirty swabs and bandages, past piles of twisted sheet, gibbering and gabbling on the beds. There were phials of liquid penicillin, bed-pans covered by crimson cloths, thermometer charts, feeding-cups. Sometimes I caught sight of a lashless unshaven face, as scaly and yellow as a bird's foot, gaping at the ceiling. The farther I moved from the door, the more oppressive became the smell, so that before I had gone half-way round the ward, I had to return to the sister.

She still hardly showed any emotion, but I could tell that she had noticed my nausea. 'Try that book,' she said softly, pointing at an exercise book on the table. 'It shows who has been moved out of here during the past three days.' As if by providence, there was Manvers' name at the top of the list, with the number of his new ward. I was about to thank her, when a man suddenly recovered consciousness, shouting, 'Ah, ah, my head, my head,' in a sobbing, throaty way and – as unflurried as ever – she moved off purposely to give him an injection.

The sister in charge of Manvers' ward was the motherly sort. Her face looked as if it were washed half-hourly with carbolic soap and cold water. She at once knew the way to his bed and asked me to follow her.

This ward was full of light and consisted of two rooms with a doorless archway between. The first was for 'old lags', as the sister put it – men who had been in hospital over eight weeks. Most were sitting bolt upright, propped up by pillows. You could see that their heads were shaved under the bandages. The eyes of nearly all of them looked glazed, and their hands lay limply on the blankets in front of them. 'Hey, Officer, I say,' an authoritative voice called to me. I turned and saw a thin parchment-skinned head on a long neck with an Adam's apple like a thorn. 'I wish to report two spiders,' this creature said, without seeming to look at me. The sister grasped me by the elbow and we walked on quickly, nearly colliding with another patient, an ambling barefooted orang-outang of a man, pursued by two Italian orderlies.

Manvers had a bandage round both ears as if he had had a mastoid operation. His eyes were shut, and yet he moved about at intervals, making tiny squeals like a dog dreaming. I had a sudden feeling that this man wasn't really Manvers at all, and that somehow the name-tabs had been switched. His eyebrows looked brown instead of black, and his complexion, once so clear and florid, was all spotty and puckered. Even his nose seemed a different shape.

To my dismay the sister shook him roughly by the shoulder, so that his head waggled on the pillow.

'Come on, Manvers, take a pull,' she said, suddenly irritated. 'Here's your officer.' As this made no impression, she soon left. For about five minutes I sat on a stool, whispering: 'Manvers, can you hear me, can you hear me? It's me, Mr. Trevelyan.' I wondered if deep down in that clouded brain he was really listening to me, but for some reason had lost those faculties that enabled him to respond. I put my mouth to one of the lumps of bandage over an ear and said slowly: 'You're all right, Manvers. You'll get better. You've got to get better.' And then I had that feeling again that Manvers wasn't lying there, and that I was only confusing this poor fellow. So I left without telling the sister, who was giving something white in a glass to the orang-outang, now safely in bed again. The man who had shouted about spiders was gently flapping his open palm in front of his face as if he were a priest about to deliver a blessing. . . .

Next I went to see Langdon. I had thought he had been killed by the spandau at the same time as Corporal Peter. A bullet had dislocated his jaw, and there were steel clamps round his teeth. All his throat was discoloured and swollen under the chin as if he had mumps. I could tell that he was pleased to see a familiar face, but he was barely able to utter one word that was intelligible.

31st May

Yesterday afternoon at four o'clock Max Factor took the piece of grenade out of my cheek. The operating theatre was on the other side of the courtyard in one of the storerooms. I walked over in my pyjamas and waited on a bench in a sort of condemned cell with a Gurkha and three South African corporals. Every ten minutes or so a sister would call a name, and one of my companions would have to lie down on a stretcher and be wrapped in a crimson blanket (so that the blood wouldn't show, the last corporal remarked) then he would be trotted out by two orderlies.

When my turn came I had to be left on the floor of the corridor until the *reliquiae* of my predecessor had been removed from the trolley. As soon as I had been wheeled into the theatre, I was surrounded by a number of yashmak'd houris, brandishing syringes and the like. They might have been taking part in *Scheherazade*, as with graceful gestures of obeisance they drew aside for the great Max Factor himself, also yashmak'd, but bare-armed and wearing rubber gloves. I was to have a local anaesthetic, he told me. Unseen hands blindfolded me, and while other hands pressed down on my legs and shoulders, I felt the prick of the needle near my cheekbone. I lay rigid, not daring to stir in case the operation started without my realizing it. Meanwhile Max Factor, after murmuring 'Take my gloves, will you?' began softly to question me about where I lived and what my father did. I answered in monosyllables, trying not to move my face muscles.

I became aware of a scratching on my cheek, as if it were canvas with a needle being dragged over it. Except for a 'Quite still now', Max Factor kept up his flow of questions, most of them demanding far more in reply than a simple yes or no. What were the advantages of Winchester over Eton? Why did I not want to make the Army my career after the war? Metal tinkled against glass; a tap was run for about twenty seconds. 'Will you be needing these?' a female voice demanded, but received no answer.

I could feel the sweat soaking into my pyjamas. I desperately wanted to grip on to something, but all I could do was to curl up my toes as tightly as possible. Then the pressure on my legs and shoulders relaxed, and I knew it was done. 'You might like to send home this piece of metal we've taken out of you,' Max Factor said to me from far away.

Then, at last, back across the courtyard on a stretcher. I had to be taken upstairs to my ward in a lift, but somebody had left a gate open and so the orderlies dumped me on the ground whilst they went to investigate. It happened that I was left outside the Clearance Ward, where I had been to look for Manvers earlier in the day. I was lying with my eyes closed when a brisk voice said: 'Gracious, it's you again.' Standing over me was the first sister to whom I'd spoken. Her eyes were narrowed in the glare. She was carrying a large dark bottle which made me notice the length and whiteness of her fingers. 'I thought you were one of the new intake,' she said, looking at me so hard that I felt embarrassed. But she was gone before I had time to give an explanation of myself.

I was sorry that she had seen me like that, with my eyes closed and my hair drenched in sweat.

The orderlies were away so long that I thought I had been forgotten. It would have been quite easy for me to get up from my stretcher and climb the stairs on foot. I was thirsty too.

A shadow crossed me and I saw that the sister was back again. 'I've brought you some barley-water,' she said, kneeling to prop my head for me.

After I had finished drinking, she took a handkerchief from her sleeve and dabbed my forehead. Her eyes were close to mine, and I saw that they were very blue, with darker, greenish markings round the pupils, like moonmountains. Neither of us spoke, and although the muscles on her face scarcely moved, I could sense that same gentleness, a kind of tenderness, in her expression.

Then the orderlies appeared, and as suddenly as before, she left.

Back in the ward, I found the piece of grenade wrapped in lint and tied with a safety-pin to my pyjama collar. It was only about half an inch long, or less, and I recognized it at once as having come from a grenade of British make. How did that Jerry get hold of the thing? But what the hell does that matter any longer. . . .

Later. – At midday today the dressing on my face was changed for a smaller and less obtrusive square of sticking-plaster, and I was given permission to spend the afternoon in Naples. I wanted to buy some presents for people at home, so I went to the Santa Lucia quarter, where I had been told that there were the best shops. Before I left for Anzio, practically all I had known of Naples – apart from the bombed quayside and overturned ships – was the Officers' Club, with glimpses of the Galleria Umberto and the Via Roma. Today it seemed to me, on my way down from the hospital, that it would be very difficult to know anything more of the place, as every tempting side alley was barred by the stencilled words OUT OF BOUNDS, or – for the benefit of those Americans who do not use such phraseology – OFF LIMITS.

The shops at Santa Lucia were much too grand, selling rings, watches, Capodimonte china, cameos, and coral necklaces. I trailed round looking in windows and finally decided that the only thing to do was to buy joke presents – one of those petunia-coloured silk scarves with *Sweetheart* or an erupting Vesuvius painted on them, or a bottle of pink scent called *Lovely Dame*, such as I had been pestered to look at on the stalls all the way down the Via Roma. It was a relief, therefore, to find a N.A.A.F.I. gift shop opposite the entrance to the Galleria, and here I bought some almonds and raisins in wooden boxes, and some stuff called *Acqua di Capri*, fantastically expensive, for Peakaboo since she had sent me her photograph when I was in the line. For Caro I bought some rubbishy lipstick and powder, the sort of things that we used to buy for school plays at Horris Hill. The girl behind the cosmetics counter had a face like an Arab's and her arms were covered with black fur. Suddenly she started screeching and pointing at the plaster on my face. '*Ferito di guerra*,' I told her priggishly. '*No, no*,' she screamed. '*Signorina arrabbiata*.' I had to slap her hand away, or she would have prodded me. '*Signorina, signorina*,' she went on, and called her friends to come and look.

Every church I tried to see inside was shut, so was the Museum. The Royal Palace had been turned into the O.R.s' N.A.A.F.I., and I didn't feel up to the Officers' Club. I therefore collapsed into a chair outside a café in the Galleria, which – since it was the siesta hour – had the appearance of a deserted railway station. While the waiter was bringing me a Lacrima Christi, I was beset by unshaven monks with placards announcing that they had been bombed out of Monte Cassino. I gave them twenty *lire*, and afterwards when I went to pay for my wine at the cash-till I found them all sitting with the waiter behind the bar, grinning their heads off and counting out piles of dirty notes.

That was the end of my charity in Naples, I decided, until a little girl confronted me. She was crying, the tears making white streaks down her face. Her clothes looked as if they had once been of good quality, and had been neatly patched and darned, although in a filthy condition. She kept snivelling after me, so in the end I gave her twenty *lire* too. Immediately she dashed away with a high-pitched gurgle, so that I knew at once that those tears had been nothing but a trick. She was joined by four or five other children, who had been following at a distance, and they all began putting out their tongues and jeering at me.

A moment later I turned a corner, and on the pavement of the Via Roma itself, I saw a heap of greyish rags out of which protruded a bare puffy foot like a claw. Then I saw the face of an old man, his mouth wide open and his eyes glassy. I was sure he was dead, but none of the passers-by took any notice. A corporal of the R.A.M.C. overtook me; without any hesitation he went up to the old man, sprinkled the rags with A.L. 63, and walked on, whistling.

The corpse of this old man (if it were a corpse), being sprinkled with lice powder by a foreigner, seemed at that moment to symbolize the Naples of 1944. Had Parthenope come to this? And surely nothing could be more degrading for a great city than to have posters everywhere, 'BEWARE V.D.' 'THIS IS A PARTICULARLY DANGEROUS AREA FOR V.D.' Opposite the San Carlo theatre, and therefore conveniently placed for both Officers' Club and the O.R.s' N.A.A.F.I. in the Palazzo Reale, is the P.A. Centre, advertising itself in bold letters for 'after sex', and farther along is its American counterpart, the Pro. Station.

But who *really* come out the worst from all this, we – the Allies – or the Neapolitans? Certainly the Neapolitans treat our weaknesses as fair game. Witness the pimps and the touts, and the little shoe-shine boys offering you their sisters up and down the Via Roma. 'Hey, Joe, eggs and cheeps?' you hear fifty dozen times a day – a sort of password inviting you to satisfy very different appetites than what these apparently innocent words would suggest.

It is impossible to find the real Naples, the *O Sole Mio* Naples, in the garish Via Roma, full of petrol fumes and chromium shops. If I were braver, I would hire some urchin to take me on a Cook's tour of the Off Limits quarters, down those dark alleys with their leaning houses, the Piranesi tufts of grass growing from the roofs, and washing slung from window to window.

Toumi would not hesitate to go exploring there, escort

or no escort. In Algiers, after we had been fortified by a black market lunch and sundry cointreaus, he often used to make me come on what he called a Pépé-le-Moko *atmosferico* hunt in the Casbah. On such occasions he would deliberately choose the smelliest and most sinister passage-way; whenever things became particularly alarming, and malevolent eyes glittered out of every murky doorway, he would reassure me by quoting from an enthusiastic local guide-book called *Mysterious Islam Life*: 'Here we are in the very heart of Algiers, a heart gently beating like that of a carefree, beautiful girl.' Another favourite quotation was: 'Get lost in the Casbah's narrow streets, allow its lure to work on you. . . .'

An unexpected find, this afternoon, outside the post office was a tray of English books, being sold by a General Smuts with a tobacco-stained beard. I felt desperately sad for him. It is the educated class that has suffered most in Naples; they still cling to their shreds of pride. You see them in the Galleria, with their scarecrow shoulders and turnip-coloured faces, hardly able to spare enough *lire* for a watered-down vermouth at one of the cafés, which anyhow to all intents have been requisitioned by the military. General Smuts never said a word to me, and I could tell that I was only causing him pain by buying a copy of a 1900 Baedeker for Southern Italy.

If Baedeker made no bones about his irritation with the Naples of 1900, how much more would he have hated it forty-four years later. 'The life of the people of Naples,' I have been reading, 'is carried on with more careless indifference to publicity than in any other town in Europe. . . . The cracking of whips, braying of donkeys, and shrill shouting of hawkers render it a most distasteful place.' Today one might substitute the rumbling of three-tonners, the grinding of brakes of fifteen hundredweights, the piercing blast of the whistle of the American military policeman, and the furtive suggestions of panders and purveyors of erotica. Baedeker is particularly solicitous about matters of health: 'The native white wines are too astringent in their action.' 'The figs of the Indian cactus are better left untouched.' 'Iron bedsteads should if possible be selected, as being less infested by the enemies of repose.' 'Masks for the face, and gloves are used to ward off the attacks of these pertinacious intruders (mosquitoes)'. But my favourite piece of guide-book advice is still one that I read in *The Curious Stranger in Bombay*: 'In the privacy of his bedroom the visitor may, if he so desire, remove all items of his clothing.'

A kind of jungle law prevails among the lower levels of the life of Naples – in other words it is the survival of the most cunning, or the least scrupulous. You are expected to know that you will be cheated, and if you cheat in return you will be esteemed the more for it. Yet you cannot be cross with a Neapolitan for long. There is a charm in his very shamelessness. It is perfectly true that, if you are the owner of a fifteen hundredweight, it is unsafe to drive through the congested traffic of the Via Roma without a guard sitting behind – otherwise boys will slit the canvas, vault inside, and steal your luggage. And still you can only laugh when you hear such stories.

One of the corporal's at Max Factor's told me that he had taken a truck on his own to collect an officer from the Transit Hotel. He had deliberately cleared everything out of the back and all his valuables were on the seat beside him in the cab. As he was waiting outside the hotel, some boys came rushing up as if in a great panic, shouting and pointing to the rear of the vehicle. He dashed round, found nothing, and on his return to the cab was in time to see the boys making off with his belongings.

Should you be fool enough to leave your car or truck unguarded, almost certainly you must expect (*a*) the petrol to be siphoned out, and (*b*) the tyres to be removed. There is a story current that, in a certain part of the Via Roma, people could not understand why their hats kept being whipped off their heads and disappearing without a trace. Then it was discovered that there was always a woman hanging around with a large basket on her head. Inside this basket she had a tiny boy. . . .

In Algiers one never found this sort of thing funny. The fact that your tent could be stolen whilst you slept, without your realizing it, never made the Arabs endearing. At the Mustapha Racecourse transit camp I had to sleep with my bedding laid over all my possessions – trunk, packs, valise, equipment, shoes – so that I should know at once if anything were pulled out from under me. You would never dare walk alone after dark along the stretch of road beyond Fort de l'Eau for fear of being 'mashed' by bandits, and this for Toumi and me was always the snag about being stationed twenty miles from Algiers without transport of our own. Once I even had to spend the night in a guardroom cell, having been stranded half-way without a hitch-hike.

In Algiers, as in Naples, you have the feeling of being buried in a kind of vibrating anthill of colourful humanity, but in Algiers this humanity is at the same time calculating and ruthless. Algiers is not a place in which to be lonely. You can be hit by such a depression as to be almost unsupportable. Toumi and I used to call it Algeriana. The night I got Algeriana most badly, and most unaccountably, was when we had just returned from a leave in Bou Saada. We had gone to have a drink at the 'secret' bar of the *Echo d'Alger* printing works, since the ordinary bars were closed at the maddeningly early hour of nine o'clock. There we found Madame Matthieu, the tennis player. All my companions were Wimbledon fans, and I – never having been to Wimbledon – soon began to feel very out of things. I sensed Algeriana looming up, and since I was also tired after an eight-hour bus ride over the Little Atlas, I decided to slip away to the transit camp – not the one on the racecourse this time, but even more incongruously in the wagons-lit coaches near the docks. The way down was through some deserted half-lighted streets, with warehouses and ordnance dumps on either side. By the time I had reached my bunk I was thoroughly in the grips of Algeriana. Then outside, among all those cranes and funnels, I heard a long-drawn-out wail of terror, as if someone had been knifed. . . .

The news bulletins are posted outside the Clearance Ward. I was standing there this evening when the new intake arrived. Stretcher after stretcher was carried through, each sending off sickly waves of that stench of life-in-death. I had to escape, but before I went I caught sight of the sister, still unruffled, perfectly in charge. Someone called her Celia. . . .

1st June

I have spent this morning sightseeing in Naples with one Ronnie Tombs of the Seaforths. I met him in the Library at the ungodly hour of 6 a.m., as we had both been turfed out of our beds at five-fifteen. Why hospitals have to do this I can never understand – it would be just as easy to put the whole routine of the place back an hour. Is it really necessary to make life hell for so many people, just so certain of the staff can be at the Club by opening time? Luckily, although getting up early has never been one of my strong points, I am not so worried by it at the moment after what I have been used to in the last months.

Ronnie has been here since April. He is suffering from a crack on the head after a shell had dropped too close to his motor bicycle at the Sangro. Although only twenty-two himself, he claims to be separated from some wealthy woman in her late thirties living at Sunningdale – so he says, you can never entirely believe Ronnie's tales, except that in this case I have had a surfeit already of the details of his sex life. He is tall – well over six foot – and covers his acne-pitted face with American talcum powder called *He-Man*; his curiously bodiless pinky-grey eyes have a squint, since he is too vain to wear glasses. One suspects, on first seeing his rather coarse lips and blond hair (always impeccably in place) that he has a touch of albino tarbrush, so to speak. Seen from behind, with his swaying walk, hunched shoulders, and elbows tight into his sides, he could have stepped straight from a pin-table saloon in the Charing Cross Road.

Ronnie is one of those people who certainly do not find the Neapolitans charming. His detestation of all things Italian is pathological. The faintest whiff of garlic, he maintains, makes him ill for days. If he sees a child urinating at a street corner, I can often barely restrain him from attacking it with the silver-knobbed cane that he always carries. All 'Wop' men, he says, look like pansies.

On more than one occasion this morning in Naples I felt so embarrassed that I nearly gave him the slip. He would take an immediate and passionate dislike to some individual and follow him down the street, making loud personal remarks, calling out: 'Hey, *pazzo*!' or '*Quanta costa*, baby?' Another favourite game was to choose the most crowded stretch of the Via Roma and start darting around, knocking into people, pretending to throw an invisible ball into the air and catching it.

I was determined to prove to him that there were plenty of redeeming features about Naples, and so with my 1900 Baedeker we set out in search of the Angevins at the Castel Nuovo, only to find that it was bombed and out of bounds. The Royal Palace and the Bourbons were next, but we weren't even allowed in by the back entrance, our way being barred not by halberdiers but by truculent bare-kneed R.A.S.C. lance-corporals. The imposing church opposite, San Francesco di Paola, was shut too. By then Ronnie was becoming exceedingly tiresome, and announced that Vivien Leigh in *Lady Hamilton* was the only figure that interested him in Neapolitan history. I had heard that the Castello dell'Ovo had appeared in the film, so we made our way there – but it also had been requisitioned, this time by the Navy. Finally we ended up in a grove of dusty palm trees, and here we stumbled upon the Aquarium, where at least we were able to see the famous octopus being prodded by an old man with a stick. Ronnie went into ecstasies over the sluggish brown bag with its suckers sticking to the glass pane. At last, he said, he had found a worthwhile reason for visiting Naples – even Vesuvius had disappointed him by not smoking and looking like any other mountain.

When he became bored by the octopus, we decided to go back to the Galleria for a vermouth. On the way Ronnie was seized with a desire to call in at the Y.W.C.A. He behaved very mysteriously, telling me to go ahead alone and sit in the room where there was a piano; he would follow shortly afterwards, but I was to pretend not to know him. Then, after he'd gone out again, I was to wait a minute or so and carefully note down the comments of the other people around me.

About half a dozen Q.A.I.M.N.S. and their escorts were having elevenses in the room. I sat down on a sofa, and a moment later Ronnie appeared at the door. He stood quite still, his white skull-face looking as if he had just given it a fresh coat of *He-Man*. Sighing loudly, he strolled across to the piano, opened it and sat down. At once a hush settled on the room, and all eyes turned expectantly towards him. Ronnie gave his head a quick shake, so that long strands of his hair fell over his eyes. He appeared to be in a kind of trance. Suddenly he braced himself and struck three loud chords. A violent arpeggio followed, as if he were embarking on some pseudo Rachmaninov prelude. But, as abruptly, he stopped, smoothed back his hair, sighed again, and walked out of the room without shutting the piano. . . .

2nd June

Oh I am in love. I am in love with Celia. I know it sounds ludicrous when we have only known each other for one evening, but it's true, I'm positive, I swear it. The whole thing came over me like a thunderclap as we drove back last night.

This love is destroying me. I feel ill with it. I can't sleep. I can't eat. Oh, God, I am like an insect on a pin. How will I ever dare tell her? She would only laugh at me. I couldn't bear that.

I must write this to ease my mind. There is nobody to tell. Celia, Celia, Celia. I love you. I love you desperately. Once before I thought I was in love, but it was never like this. . . .

I have all the classical symptoms. I wish I could laugh at myself, but I feel too ill – not in my heart, but deep down inside somewhere. Last night I turned on my bed for hours, threw off my blanket, pulled it over me again; opened the curtains to let in more air, drew them back when the light outside shone on my face; went for a drink of water, but ten minutes later was scorched by a raging thirst; asked for aspirins, then again for more two hours later; counted sheep, the ticking of a clock. But none of these were of any use. I only think of *you*; and when we were called at five-fifteen I was still awake.

My head is in splints of iron. I have no energy. To revive myself I must pass by your ward in the hope of catching some quick glimpse of you. You are a necessary drug. What can I do to make you love me? Can I give you presents? I don't even know your tastes, what sort of things you like. To you I am only another patient in this hospital, temporary, a bird of passage. Is there no small errand I can run for you? I dare not seem persistent in case I lose what little ground has been gained between us. . . .

Oh, God, this is agony. I have never known such torment. *The torment of love unsatisfied.* How I ache to touch the back of your hand, your shoulder, nothing more. I would not dare go further without encouragement. I should die if you repelled me.

You said we might 'run into one another' at the Club again tonight. Does that mean that you would *like* to see me there? I don't know if I could bear to see you being happy with someone else.

Just give me one sign that there is hope for me, the tiniest gesture. I will wait for it, in the heat, in the cold, in the rain, in the sirocco. . . .

This is how it happened. Yesterday in the afternoon I went out again with Ronnie. We had an hour or so to kill before going to *Madama Butterfly* at the San Carlo. Ronnie decided that he wanted to do his Rachmaninov stunt again at the Y.W.C.A. When I went into the piano room, the only person there was Celia, sitting on the sofa. She was dressed in civilian clothes, in a plain green dress with a white collar.

On the spur of the moment I asked if I could sit beside her. I hardly thought she would recognize me. She looked up with a faint lifting of the eyebrows, as though amused, almost condescending. When she spoke, it was in that curious cool tone that she had employed when I had first met her in the Clearance Ward. 'If you like,' was all she said. 'But I'm waiting for someone.'

Ordinarily I would have felt chilled or shy. In uniform she had looked only a bit older than myself, but I now realized that she must be in her late twenties. For the first time, too, I realized how beautiful she was – but such a pale *sad* beauty, as though carved in marble. The structure of her face was almost too smoothly perfect, but in some odd way I think it was her hair, absolutely without a wave or curl, that drew me to her first; and of course her eyes.

I had barely seated myself when Ronnie appeared. Although obviously peeved that his audience was so small, he put plenty of gusto into his performance. Only after he'd left did Celia throw her head back and laugh. I was taken aback, mainly because at that time laughter was out of keeping with the opinion of her that I'd built up for myself. I noticed that there were tears in her eyes. 'Poor, poor Ronnie,' she said, gasping. 'He had to go through with it, even though he knew I'd seen that trick a dozen times before.' Then I laughed too, and immediately whole mountains crumbled away between us. She told me that Ronnie was the laughing-stock of the 186th; they were wondering whether to ship him back to the U.K. Then we went on to all sorts of other topics. I told· her about the dismal failure of our sightseeing trip that morning and how we were going to *Madama Butterfly*. She said that she was waiting to be taken out to tea at Harold Macmillan's villa at Posillipo by 'a sort of uncle' from A.F.H.Q.

All of a sudden I remembered that Ronnie was waiting for me outside in the street.

He was livid. I had 'insulted' him by making him hang around as if he were waiting to pick up a Wop tart. Why didn't I warn him that there was only one person in the room? And Celia Marchant of all people; he'd never hear the end of it from the other sisters. He was sulking all the time we sat in a bar in the Galleria, and at the beginning of each interval at the opera he rushed out without speaking to me.

The San Carlo, all crimson, white and gilt, with its tiers of boxes glittering with lights reflected in the mirrors, must be the doyen of opera houses the world over. At last we could conjure up the Bourbons, but Ronnie affected not to hear when I told him this. Already my mind was disturbed by Celia. Perhaps it was because of her that my attention kept wandering during the opera, or perhaps it was mainly because, in the caustic words of Baedeker, 'silence during the performance of music is never very strictly observed'. Two things about that *Madama Butterfly* will always stay in my mind. One was the device for suggesting fireflies on the stage, consisting of nothing more than a branch of spangles waved by a ghostly hand from behind cardboard bushes. The other was the sight of a little girl in ringlets who sat alone in one of the most sumptuous of the boxes. She was ushered in by a footman in crimson and white livery, matching the colour-scheme of the theatre, and allowed this man to stand at attention behind her until such time as she saw fit to dismiss him. At first she sat bolt upright, every inch a born duchess, but the moment the lights went out, she put on glasses and hung over the edge of the box just like any other little girl.

After the opera Ronnie and I went into the Officers' Club next door, as we'd decided to have dinner there. The bar was already packed with people swilling down gin fizzes and leopard's breath (vermouth and cognac). Ronnie found some members of his regiment and went off

144

to join them. It was then that I noticed Celia with a bucolic R.E.M.E. captain at the other end of the bar. This time she was wearing uniform. The captain was without any doubt half-seas-over and was talking volubly into her face. She seemed magnificently bored. I caught her eye and she waved, at which the captain wheeled round with indignant little porker's eyes.

The strains of *Funiculi Funicula* could be heard in the distance, and since this was the signal for the opening of the restaurant, nearly everyone began to drift away, including Celia and her captain. I collected Ronnie, who had temporarily forgotten our contretemps, and we found a table about four away from Celia's.

Ronnie at once began to irritate me by being excessively rude to the Italian waiters, who he said had disgusting fingernails and weren't fit to touch the plates we ate off. Then he said that the soup tasted of garlic and sent it back to the kitchens. When more soup was brought he said that he'd decided not to have any after all. Next he turned his attention to the dancers, and in a penetrating voice began criticizing various aspects of their anatomies. Finally, when a great raven-haired soubrette came to the microphone and began singing 'Boum' and 'Ciribiribin', he ostentatiously clapped his hands to his ears, declaring that she was notorious for having been the mistress of a German field-marshal and that it was a disgrace that she was allowed to sing in a British officers' club.

By the time the band had started to play 'The Blue Danube' I was feeling considerably more than bored by Ronnie's behaviour. I also had an overpowering urge to go on the floor (probably because a Viennese waltz is about the only dance I pride myself on being able to do). Celia's captain was just lurching off to the loo, so without a word of explanation to Ronnie, I went over and asked her to dance.

I knew she was relieved to be away from the captain. 'We both seem to have struck unlucky with our companions,' I ventured as we started off. She stiffened. 'What do you mean?' she asked, so frostily that I was startled. I apologized, saying that I had forgotten that she was meeting her uncle. 'Oh, for goodness' sake,' she said. 'I was only joking. He's not really my uncle.'

I felt unhappy, groping about in my mind for a different topic. It seemed as if we were strangers again. I told her about Ronnie's petulance since our meeting at the Y.W.C.A. and how he wouldn't speak to me at the San Carlo. Suddenly she burst into laughter, throwing her head back just as she had done the first time. The spell was broken. I waltzed as never before. I don't know what we talked about – it's difficult to talk when you're waltzing – but we always seemed to be laughing. It was like being in a singing top. Other people revolved dizzily past in one long streamer of pink, white and khaki. A hundred times, miraculously, we missed collisions. We were possessed by a delicious frenzy. Only her face was in focus for me.

We felt so giddy when the music stopped that we had to stand still, supporting one another. Celia looked quite different with her eyes sparkling and her cheeks full of colour. I had never seen anyone so beautiful. She was still laughing. I held her by the arm as we swayed back to the table.

The R.E.M.E. captain had already returned. He was very drunk, and I could see masses of tiny veins like purple wire-worms on his nose. We were not prepared for his aggressiveness. 'What the — hell do you think you're up to, you — twerp?' he shouted thickly so that everyone at the surrounding tables looked at us. I told him not to be silly and to mind his language. 'I'll learn you — silly,' he bellowed, hauling himself up to his feet. I realized too late that he was going to rip the dressing off my face, and he

146

would have done so had not Celia smacked his hand away in the nick of time. I could see she was blazing. 'You revolt me,' she spat out. 'Now sit down.' She pushed him, and he slumped, suddenly meek, into a chair. She signalled that I should leave.

Ronnie greeted me with a sardonic grimace. 'So you've decided to chase our Sister Celia. You won't get very far with her. She's what's known as pachydermatous – the bitch with the toughest hide in Naples.' My temper is very seldom roused to boiling point, but this time I really let him have it. At the end Ronnie said nothing, but stood up, white-faced, and left without paying his bill.

I stayed on alone for about half an hour. Now and then I glanced at Celia, and each time I saw that she had her back half-turned on the captain and was watching the dancers. Another Viennese waltz struck up. A thin Scots Guards subaltern with a clipped moustache was dancing with a woman in civilian clothes; she had very fat legs, and her hair, which had been piled like a loaf on her head, became unpinned and fell over her neck. They waltzed round and round with fantastic vigour, quite oblivious of the rest of the room. Soon, because of the heat, all the other couples left the floor, but the thin subaltern and the fat-legged woman went on dancing, staring as though en-tranced at one another. Some people began to cheer, but still these two didn't seem to notice. I wondered if Celia and I had looked as absurd as that, and involuntarily I turned towards her. The captain was bent forward with his forehead on the table; evidently he had passed out. Celia was gathering her things together.

She walked across to me. 'I'm going,' she said curtly. 'Would you like a lift to the hospital? Bill's got a staff car outside, and I shall make his driver take me home.'

In the car I could sense her fury still simmering inside her. By way of making conversation I asked where she lived in England. She said she didn't come from England, but from Ireland – County Carlow – adding that it was 'donkey's years' since she'd been able to get back there. She told me this with a faint tremor, and then remarked that she had had a brother called Dermot, who had been in my regiment and who had been killed at Calais. She loathed the 186th and had only volunteered to come to Italy so that she could be transferred to Rome, where she had once spent a year as a child.

Now she had dropped her 'professional' tone again. I was conscious that she trusted me – not in the sense that she knew I wouldn't make a clumsy pass at her (as so many girls of my own age would have expected me to do), but in a quite different way. I was glad that her brother had been in my regiment, as this established a small bond between us.

She began to tell me about the tea-party at Harold Macmillan's, and about the view of Sorrento and Capri from Posillipo. I sat back, listening. The streets were nearly deserted. We were alone, she and I, in the back of the car, gliding alone through this incredible city, and suddenly my love broke out in a great incandescent flame. My whole body was filled with such wild joy to be close to her. I felt strangely light-headed, as if we were spinning round in that waltz again. The force with which I had been hit was almost more than I could stand. It was as though I had been sucked up by a vast tidal wave, and flung down mercilessly on a beach of rocks and shingle. . . .

The news bulletins give me plenty of excuses for lingering outside Celia's ward. I see that the Moletta has been crossed the whole way along. Ardea is in our hands. Rome should fall any day now.

They tell me that tomorrow I am to be sent to the Convalescent Home at Sorrento. I shall be there six days, then I am to come back for a night to the 186th. . . .

A hundred and forty-four hours apart. Almost I am in love in spite of myself. She is older, more experienced in life; I know almost nothing about her. I try to tell myself that less than two weeks ago I was still at Anzio, that this has only happened because I *admire* her for her competence and self-control, because she is the first person since Anzio to have been kind to me and to have shown me affection – but it's no use. I have not been more certain of anything in all my life. . . .

This love is no happiness for me. Sometimes I think I shall touch madness with the pain of it. It is like some obscure illness eating up my brain. It is like the lava in the crater of Vesuvius. I wish I could write you a letter of such molten heat as would send the whole of that blessed Clearance Ward hurtling across the bay and into the aeons. . . .

Am I a coward for not declaring myself to you? I want to be *certain* first that you can love me too. Last night, as we walked back from the Club, I was bursting to tell you how I felt. We talked so frankly. Did you have any inkling of the torture I was going through?

Your eyes seem to say that you love me, but I cannot be sure. There are times when you smile at me and I feel that I have gained slightly in your favour, and that there is hope. But hope for what? Dare I hope that you will ever love me as I love you? I have never been devoured so utterly by a single passion. You admitted last night that you had already been in love. You said that having loved once, you could never truly love again. You then said that if one's first love is brought to disappointment, in time one realizes that there will always be another love beyond, even though it will lack that original intensity. In a way I would like to believe this, so that my love for you, if it is to be without fulfilment, will remain for ever the most sacred of my memories.

Last night, when we parted, we counted the hours until we would meet again. I knew then that you do look forward to being near me. You said that you would wait for me at nine o'clock outside the notice board. Now, as I write this in the Library, it is only eight o'clock. Oh, God, make this next hour pass quickly. . . .

I am so conscious of my own faults. You are so beautiful; how can I dare suppose that you should ever want to love me? I want to please you in every trivial thing. Is my hair cut too long? Are my trousers well enough creased? Have I any mannerisms you dislike? Just say if there is anything about me that offends you.

If you were to ask this sort of question about yourself, I would not know how to answer. To me everything about you is perfection, whatever you wear, however you feel. I love you composed and cool as when I first met you. I love you when your hair is out of place. I love you in uniform. I love you in that green dress. I love you. I love you. I love you. The thought of having to go to Sorrento is a black nightmare to me. . . .

My clothes are strewn about the bed, as I sort them out for Sorrento. I cannot do anything more until I have seen your name written down in front of me. Celia – there I've done it. Celia. I would like to cover this page with hundreds of thousands of Celias. Celia, Celia, I love you. Celia, Celia, I love you – like that, over and over again.

This is so unfair. Being in love should stabilize me.

Instead I am tossed from one emotion to another. When you are away from me I am sent head over heels down into the cold chasms, and there I stay, bumping painfully along the bottom, until I so much as catch a single glimpse of you and once more I am sailing high up among the clouds again.

I dread the future, but perhaps I dread the past even more. Who is this man you loved? How much did you love him? I cannot help deliberately torturing myself with thoughts like these. I would have liked you to have remained pure, untouched, untouchable until I met you.

I cannot sleep these nights because of thinking of you. My eyes are aching. My nerves are on edge. Only being with you *always* will bring me rest. . . .

If only I could confide in someone. Ronnie is useless. I could never trust him, and besides, he hates you, even though he did apologize for the other night. Love is not a thing to be kept secret. My dearest, how I long to hear from your own lips that you love me too, so that together we can shout our news from the roof tops of the Vomero. . . .

A year ago, on 21st March to be exact, I became engaged. The whole thing only lasted fifteen days, but how lucky both for Catherine and for me that we realized our mistake before it was too late – or rather that Catherine realized our mistake and broke it off. I would like to tell you about how this came about, so that you will know that only my love for *you* is genuine, and that I have never really been in love before.

Catherine and I were children together, the same age. We were inseparable companions, spending as much of our holidays as we could in each other's company. The bond between us became so strong that we said that we could carry on 'dumb' conversations – Catherine could ask me a question and I could reply without our having to open our mouths. Catherine left school when she was seventeen, and consequently was in the world long before I was. Then she started her first affair, and ingenuously she relayed all the details on to me. Soon I became frantically jealous, for I had already come to the romantic conclusion that we were predestined for one another. I tried to hint at this in my letters, but Catherine never appeared to understand. This went on until March last year when she told me about some Cherry Picker, who was so 'intriguing' – all Catherine's young men were intriguing – and I, in the flush of my newly-gained commission, blurted out that I was jealous. And so we became engaged.

Two weeks later it was all over and Catherine went back to her Cherry Picker for good. I was terribly hurt at the time, but now that I have met you, I know that it was my pride that was wounded, not my heart.

2 *p.m.* Ronnie, attempting to make amends invited me to the Club for a drink before lunch. But a shadow had fallen between us, and there were none of his ball-throwing games in the Via Roma.

At the Club I found Nigel Mount and Dicky Longhilton. It was exciting to meet some members of my own regiment again, although I'd never particularly cared for either of these two. They told me that there is a good chance of my being transferred to one of our battalions, so at least there is some future in sight when I leave Sorrento. Dicky offered me a couple of tickets for *Traviata* at the San Carlo this evening. He said the seats were specially good. Of course I accepted at once, and now Ronnie is offended again because I mean to take Celia instead of him.

On my return to hospital I couldn't find Celia at her ward. I therefore had to leave a note for her with Carmine, the Italian orderly there.

I've just had a letter from Simon. It only took thirty-six hours to reach me from the Front. He says that Jim Eagle insisted on going up to the Fortress to look round after the Jerries had been cleared out. In particular Jim wanted to see that position where Mike held out so wonderfully, and on his way there had stepped straight on to a pencil mine.

Simon was indignant about the recruits who were given to the Battalion after the Moletta Crossing; not, he admits, that it was Div. H.Q.'s fault. All the recruits were completely raw and very young, with no battle experience. Less than a day after their arrival they had to be flung straight into the attack, with disastrous consequences.

4th June

6.30 a.m. Oh, God, what has happened? I am utterly wretched.

I know I have no right to expect her to love me, but need she have behaved quite so callously? This afternoon I go to Sorrento, and I shall leave plunged in misery and uncertainty. Last night I thought the whole world would yawn apart.

Several times yesterday after lunch I passed her ward, hoping for a reply to my message about *Traviata*. A batch of bad casualties had arrived, so each time she was too busy to see me. I was not able to find Carmine either.

The opera started at 6 p.m. I waited outside the Sisters' quarters until five forty-five, but still there was no sign of Celia. Even if we managed to get a lift to the San Carlo, we would have arrived after the curtain had gone up. I sent word to ask if Sister Marchant were in her room, and to let her know that I was waiting. The reply

153

horrified me. Sister Marchant was inside, but was very sorry that she had no time to see me.

The blood roared in my head. I was stunned. At first I could not believe that I had heard correctly. In a grey emptiness I walked to the hospital gates. There was no question now of going to the opera.

As I turned into the street, a horn sounded behind me. It was the R.E.M.E. captain's staff car, and in the back was Celia, alone. She waved.

I must have visited every bar in the Galleria. I had nothing to eat, as I couldn't face the Club, and the civilian restaurants were too expensive. Then I met a French officer called André, who asked me to come with him to the Colorado. He was drunk too, as he was going to lead a drop on the Haute Savoie the next day.

The Colorado is supposed to be the only decent hot-spot in Naples. As it is for French officers only, you are not allowed in without an invitation. Immediately we arrived we were surrounded by hostesses. André insisted that I should have first pick, so I chose one called Teresa with two white carnations in her hair.

Teresa was nice to me. We danced a good deal, and once I kissed her behind her Spanish fan. At the end of the evening she seemed to assume that as a matter of course I would come home with her. I protested that I was *ferito* and had to be in hospital. Well, then, the next night, she said. But I was going to Sorrento. When would I be back? Tuesday? All right, she'd wait for me until Tuesday night. So, glad to escape, I left it at that.

André took me back to hospital in his jeep. He had a girl with him, and I heard him tell the driver to call him at two-thirty. . . .

11.30 *a.m.* Now it is over. I have seen Celia. She says we must not see one another any more. She *cannot* under-stand what this means.

154

At least we have cleared up last night's misunderstanding. That wretch Carmine never gave her my note. She didn't even know I wanted her to come with me to *Traviata*.

When we met an hour ago, it was no longer possible to hide what I felt. She must have guessed the truth already before I told her, but – oh, the effort to drag out the words *I love you* for the first time face to face – worse still, because I could see quite plainly that I had been wrong, that she did not love me in return.

Then it was done. There was nothing else I could say, and since we were in the Library, where we might have been surprised at any moment, it was all the more of an anti-climax. I would have liked to behave melodramatically, to have grovelled at her feet, begged for some flicker of pity.

She told me that she had already been married. Her husband had been killed in the Battle of Britain. She also told me that the R.E.M.E. captain had been his uncle.

Now she is expecting to marry someone else, who is a P.O.W. That's the real reason why she wants to go to Rome. She feels that it will be easier to reach this man from there when the Allies advance into Germany.

She asked me how old I was. When I told her, she only laughed and said that made it all the more ridiculous. Did I know that she was over half my age again? I protested that it made no difference, that I knew my love for her was completely true, that I would kill myself if I had to go to Sorrento, never to see her again. I begged her to meet me on Tuesday and to let me write to her. She said that if I did write, she would not open my letters. . . .

I can no longer think coherently. I am torn apart like a piece of rotten calico. Nothing but bitter loneliness is ahead.

SORRENTO

6th June. Officers' Convalescent Home, Sorrento: Villa Tamara

THE news overwhelms. Yesterday Rome fell. Today the Second Front started – the moment we have longed for all these years. We were awoken at 6 a.m. by the Ligurian housemaid Guiseppina, who tore into the bedrooms, ripping aside mosquito nets and yelling: '*Bellezza* ev'rybodee, *bellezza* ev'rybodee.' Then she started hiccoughs on the landing. Servants came running to calm her, and only then did we learn what had happened. Soon we were crowded round the wireless. Although the bulletins told us nothing, the war might almost have been over. We hardly bothered about breakfast, and dashed round wildly, singing and whistling. . . .

By nine o'clock I was on the beach. The way down is through a grove of the most primeval olives I have ever seen; the trunks are twisted and hollow, all knobbles and brown jugulars. Then you pass under a ruined archway, made of bricks in herring-bone pattern, once part of a Roman villa. They say this villa must have stood on artificial piles over the sea, and it is still possible to make out traces of a grotto. The bottom of the cove is shingle, which makes the water unbelievably clear – and blue; I shall never be nasty about coloured postcards any more.

I am thankful not to be in the main Convalescent Home, in Sorrento itself at the Vesuvio-Palace Hotel.

That vast Drayton Gardensish building, with so much magenta bougainvillaea, depresses me, and there are too many people in it I know. The day after my arrival from Naples I was transferred here to the Villa Tamara, two miles out on the road to Massalubrense. Gerard Fescue and Julian Holt, both of my Regiment, are at the Palace, but I feel I must be on my own these next few days.

The Villa Tamara is no beauty, just a square white doll's house in a neat garden of geraniums, roses, azaleas and syringa. From a distance you see it sitting, a little pertly, high on this sun-reddened, cicada-haunted promontory, whose very bareness makes the sea and sky by contrast such a tremendous, arrogant blue. Behind, in the valleys, are the lemon trees, where there are fireflies by night, and before us is the whole stretch of the Bay of Naples, from the mauve humps of Vesuvius to the islands of Ischia and Procida. On the left is Capri, tantalizingly close and – ever since I have been here – all woven about by mists. Last night I sat on the terrace under the vines. The breeze was still warm, and smelt of jasmine and syringa. I watched the bay turn to silver and the lights of Naples start to glimmer and flash along the waterfront. ... And yet the whole time I was only *half* there, like watching a trailer on the cinema screen. Perhaps I have come to this too suddenly.

A Mrs. Randolph runs the Villa on what one might call country house lines. She knew my parents eight years ago in Nowshera, but I'm not sure if she cares to be reminded of this, as it puts us into different generations. She wanders about, pink, portly, and wide-eyed, with huge bunches of cannas, or lies in basket-chairs drinking iced vermouth and soda. Her pet topic is the dust everywhere – caused by the recent eruption of Vesuvius – and no wonder, since she only likes to wear pastel-coloured dresses. It is true that she succeeds very well in making

157

you forget the Army. I felt so warm towards her yesterday for having achieved this, that I wanted to give her a present; all I could think of was a typically Army relic – that pair of surgeon's scissors I took off the German warrant officer at the Moletta Crossing.

There are, in fact, at least seven members of my Regiment, including Gerard and Julian, convalescing at the Palace Hotel. All have suffered the same nonchalant treatment as I – doled out to any regiment that happened to be short of officers – and are now hoping to be posted to one of our own battalions. As Gerard acidly remarked, you have to get yourself wounded if you want to stay in the Regiment. Julian made a great show of being put out because I was so patently pleased to be able to escape to the Tamara. He took me to meet the family of the great philosopher Benedetto Croce, who has a villa more or less on the site of where Tasso lived. I was at once asked, the moment I set foot inside the house, whether I was a relation of G. M. Trevelyan. Well, yes, I said, but unfortunately not all that close. This admission may have been too disappointing for them, or perhaps they genuinely did misunderstand me; the fact is that they are all now firmly under the impression that I am his nephew. It was as such that I was introduced to Alberto Moravia and his wife, also staying at the villa. Even the sage, Croce himself, was brought downstairs in order to say a few words to me in French about my 'uncle'. Until that day (and thank God nobody realized it) I had never heard of Benedetto Croce or Alberto Moravia! It was like presiding over a meeting at the Royal Society under false pretences.

After bathing this morning I lay on the beach and read. Barely half an hour had passed when I heard myself hailed from out to sea. It was Gerard and Julian in a boat belonging to Salvatore, the old fisherman at the Palace, with three of the Croce daughters, Elena, Alda and Silvia. I could not refuse to join them, and – in my phase of despising all things military – was flattered when Elena said that she had thought I was Italian, with my dark glasses and hair combed straight back (and, no doubt, my pair of very native-looking bathing-trunks, bought in the Via Roma).

Julian bored us all by holding forth about Dante in his execrable Italian. We knew he was showing off in front of Alda, the blue-stocking of the family and reputed to be her father's *alter ego*. Elena made one or two attempts to change the subject in English, but was almost shouted down; she is the eldest of the Croce girls, and is married to a leading light in the Partisans, their two children still being in the north of Italy. The only person who seemed grateful for Julian's monologue was Silvia, the shy one, a sort of southern Emily Brontë, awkwardly trailing one hand in the sea.

Eventually it was I who took advantage of a pause whilst Julian was searching for a passage in his copy of the *Inferno*. I made some banal remark about the peacefulness of the bay compared to what must be going on in Normandy. Elena shrieked at me: 'My goodness, do you mean you've been sitting here all the time and haven't thought to tell us that the Second Front has started? Now I do know you are an Englishman!' Salvatore was ordered to row straight back to their villa, the Tritone, and thus I had the distinction of being responsible for the breaking of the news to the entire Croce household. In order to retrieve some shreds of face, I gave Elena three boxes of N.A.A.F.I. matches, the sort that are unobtainable for civilians nowadays.

As we were helping the girls out of the boat on to the slippery landing stage below the Tritone, an argument blew up between Julian and Salvatore – I think about money. Suddenly, in a deliberate histrionic manner, Julian slapped the old man's face. But that was not the end of it, and Julian was still shouting at him as Gerard and I, shrivelled up with embarrassment, deposited the Croces at their gate and sneaked off unobserved to a quiet lunch on our own. We went to the Semiramis, the only unrequisitioned hotel at Sorrento.

I ate two things for the first time: raw ham and melon, and fried octopus. Gerard introduced me to a Neapolitan princess and her daughters, Madelina and Antonina, who are spending the summer at the Semiramis. All three are great, lazy, tawny things, with long, fluffy hair. We nick-named them Tigrina, Leopardina, and Panterina. They live in a superbly feline way too, all eating and sleeping: never up before eleven-thirty, then down to the beach by the hotel lift; a short swim perhaps, and sunbathing until lunch at two; siesta until five-thirty or six; tea; a gentle promenade in the town; dinner, followed by sitting on the terrace until bedtime.

I wanted to buy a box of inlaid wood for my mother. We went into the main piazza, lined with oleanders, and there found Julian involved in another row, this time with the driver of a cart. It seemed that, whilst dodging a street cleaner's hose, he had been nearly run down by this man's mule, one of those sad skinny creatures bedizened with plumes and bells and with a painted leather hump on its back as a protection against the Evil Eye. No sooner had he spied us across the piazza than Julian shouted that we had deserted him 'shamefully', adding: 'It's all down in my diary, you know.' The driver took this opportunity of making off, cracking his whip loudly in Julian's ear.

In the inlaid wood shop I bought myself a stout pair of apostolic-looking sandals and a silk handkerchief of my favourite colour, *sang-de-boeuf*, to wear as a scarf in Desert Rat fashion. Gerard kept muttering about having to find 'a really good skin food', but appeared to find nothing that pleased him. All the while we had Julian vociferously in tow. Finally I was constrained to have tea alone with him at the Palace.

Julian is a real bundle of complexes. I suppose he must be thirty-two. At first sight you might take him to be Dutch; he is smallish, with very round ears, and thin pale lips. His trouble is that he is constantly, desperately, in search of someone who can admire him – hence those bursts of temper and the hot air about Dante. Purely in order that I should be impressed, he told me that last night he took Beryl, one of the Red Cross girls, down to the beach and kissed her in the moonlight. He had a ruminative, faraway look as he said this, the way I feel in woods sometimes, when my bowels begin to stir. But I knew instinctively that he was not telling the truth; behind it all was the well-known fact that Beryl is the most sought-after female in Sorrento.

I stayed on at the Palace until sunset in order to see the famed *raggio verde*, or green ray, as the sun went down (Gerard thinks it is called the *ragioniere verde,* meaning green clerk; I've given up trying to correct him). Julian left me on the hotel balcony, which sticks out over the vertical cliff like a box at the theatre. He had given me a volume of Browning from the Red Cross library, so that I could read *The Englishman in Italy*. How it bored me. I do think that people swallow much too much of Browning without complaint. That metre. The poem might have been written by someone who'd never been out of England. This, too:

> *And then will the flaxen-winged Image*
> *Be carried in pomp*
> *Thro' the plain, while in gallant procession*
> *The priests mean to stomp.*

On the endpaper of the book was inscribed 'Gift of the B.R.C.S. and Order of St. John Hospital Library, Chugford and Brampton-le-Stoke Depot'. Visions of tweed-skirted county ladies! It takes me back to raw mornings at Little Canfield Moat, packing woollie scarves for torpedoed merchant seamen.

After sunset the breeze disappeared, and the sea became smooth, the colour of moonstones. The few boats floated just as Piranesi used to draw them mucking about on the Tiber. On the opposite side of the bay, the soft improbable skyline began to melt into a deep-blue haze – so many bays and inlets, prominences and peaks; Baiae was there, and Cumae, Bauli and the Phlegraean Fields; Cape Misenum, and somewhere beyond, Lake Avernus; then Herculaneum and Pompeii, still in awe of the silent Vesuvius. It was an evening that Turner might have dreamt about.

In the nearest boat a fisherman, pulling in his nets, began to sing, real operatic tenor stuff. He was doing it for effect, we all knew that. People flocked out of the bar on to the balcony. Now we were in Hollywood, the Italy of the Tottenham Court Road typist, and it was superb. The song had just the right mixture of jauntiness and melancholy. I asked the Cameronian next to me what it was. ' "Lili Marlene",' he said.

Still no news of the landings in Normandy. Our first excitement has crystallized into a state of anguished suspense.

7th June. Villa del Fauno, Anacapri

Midnight on Capri. Not a sound outside. Even the crickets are quiet here. Wistaria covers the dome of the house opposite, separated from us by a hedge of prickly pears.

I am too sleepy to write much. Maybe this is as well; it would be light again before I could finish describing all I have seen and done today.

Julian telephoned at breakfast. The Moravias were just off to Capri. They wanted us to join them for two nights in a friend's villa at Anacapri, where there was a spare room. When I hesitated, Julian flew off the handle. He was leaving the Convalescent Home at the end of the week. I might never see him again; he would be sent straight up to the Front and probably get killed. And, anyhow, he'd squared the Commandant.

Aimée Randolph had no objection, so within the hour I was on the R.A.F. launch outside the Cocumella Hotel. We had to go disguised as civilians, since Capri is an American Air Corps rest camp, and strictly out of bounds to Limeys except for day visits.

There were flying fish on the way. The launch took us straight to the Blue Grotto, where a score of little boats were bobbing outside the entrance, selling straw hats and coral necklaces. The great cliffs overhead, with birds wheeling round, reminded me of a print I'd once seen of Tierra del Fuego.

And then inside the Grotto. How shall I describe that blue? The colour of the cloak of a Bellini Madonna, but infinitely more translucent? Perhaps the glory of it all was that we were quite alone in there; ours was the only boat.

We chipped growing coral off the rocks. I dived into a shoal of glinting fish, and when I looked at my legs, they had turned to crystal. I saw stalactites, and was shown where Nero (so the boatman said) had his torches of burning Christians.

Next we sailed round to the Faraglioni, where we found someone who must have been a genuine maiden aunt, complete with smock and sombrero, painting in water-colours. The last time I had seen the Faraglioni was from the *Ville d'Oran* with Toumi, when we sailed past in February on our way from Algiers.

In the afternoon I walked with Alberto Moravia to the top of the Migliara, nine hundred feet above the sea (he still thinks I'm G. M. Trevelyan's nephew, which slightly makes me feel I oughtn't to be here at all). The mountainside was covered with genista. The sea looked so placid, but the rocks were like jagged molars. A place famous for suicides, said Alberto, and no wonder.

So far I have spent very little time in the town itself of Capri (or should one call it village?). In the miniature piazza, like a setting for the *Barber of Seville*, we had to jostle our way through the usual scrum of importunate *carrozza* drivers, restaurant touts, and sellers of funny hats and 'lucky' bells of San Michele. The G.I. occupation was much in evidence, every café and restaurant throbbing with dance music at the height of the siesta hour. One restaurant had a notice outside which said: 'Come on in, folks. Jus' a lil' bit of ole New York.'

Up here in Anacapri you have the direct contrast: sleepy and unspoilt, few shops. It is almost like being in North Africa, with these old whitewashed houses, flat roofs and outside staircase. Our host is Commendatore Faiella. He was until recently mayor of Anacapri. His wife is Norwegian, so the house is full of scrubbed woodwork, with blue floral pottery laid out on shelves. Francis Brett Young's villa is across the way.

We complimented the Commendatore on the beauty and serenity of the place. Yes, he said, the Villa del Fauno is *graziosa*. Julian translated *graziosa* as gracious, but the dictionary gives the meaning as pretty. Yet gracious is the best word for describing the Commendatore's house and garden.

Julian has behaved tolerably well since we arrived. It seems that Alberto has come here mainly to write. He and

Elsa escaped from Rome in September and spent the winter and spring hiding in a cowshed near Fondi, to find themselves caught neatly between Cassino and Anzio. They both look ill-fed and yellow. Alberto has a curious twist to his face, which makes him seem perpetually in pain; he also has a limp, the result of some illness in his youth. It is difficult not to brag when he starts talking about his privations and the bombardments. 'And almost all we had to read was the Bible,' he said, as if we ought to have thrown up our hands in dismay. This evening I found him writing an article on the typewriter. I glimpsed the words: *'Non ho mai visto ridere un soldato tedesco* (I have never seen a German soldier laughing).' Nor have I, but I have *heard* them laughing often enough, at the Fortress.

9th June. Villa Tamara, Sorrento

On my return from Capri this evening I found a scribble from Toumi. He had come over yesterday from Benevento, and Aimeé Randolph had put him up in my bed. He says he has been watching the shores of Capri all morning 'like the full medieval gentleman in a turret, waiting for the return of the Crusaders'. But he had to leave here after lunch.

There is a p.s. to his note, which reads: 'Stopped my chariot at Pompeii to call on that old bag Flavia. She was mad about my new toga. (Those sandals from Copula's pinch dreadfully.) Virgil is coming to stay, so they're in for a literary week-end. Epidius Rufus sends love.'

Toumi would have liked the name of the owner of the motor boat in which Julian and I left Capri – Ippolito Archimede. The boat was hired specially for us by the Commendatore, and as we left the Marina Grande children threw down cherries and flowers of rambler roses.

Julian had also brought a bag of cherries, which I absently began to eat as we cut through the velvety water. Soon the houses had become like so many pink and white dice, and we could barely make out the funicular running up and down from the piazza; it was then that Julian turned abruptly on me and said: 'How old are you?' I told him twenty. He seemed nonplussed. 'I thought you were twenty-eight,' he said. Then after a moment: 'But that explains a lot,' and he snatched the bag away from me. I laughed, which was obviously unpopular. An electric five minutes followed. 'Raleigh' (I dreaded that deliberate, quavering tone), 'I think it would do you good if I read aloud from my diary.' 'Really, Julian,' I said. 'Must it be now?' But he was not to be put off. He had a way of sticking out his chin with his head on one side. I was like a piano, apparently, sometimes in tune, sometimes not. Julian was the player – after that I didn't bother to listen. There was so much to watch, to remember, and to think about.

Of all the characters I met the one that will stick longest in my mind will be Franzie. He belonged, he told us within the first five minutes, to a family *fort ancienne,* and could trace direct descent from the brother of Attila the Hun. Indeed, he looked not unlike what Attila might have been: shaggy eyebrows over burning yellow eyes, hair cropped, unshaven chin covered with duelling scars, and a smelly shirt that from a distance looked like chain mail, but in reality was made of loosely woven cords of grey silk; he also went barefoot. Obviously he was living very near the edge. The furniture seemed good, most of it English, but was unpolished and covered with dust. Even the tea tasted of dust. He talked impulsively and rapidly in French – too rapidly for me to understand – about art, erotic symbolism in nineteenth-century poetry, original sin, and goodness knows what else. I felt like that Mrs.

Cratchmar-Baines after her nephew's talk on *Time and Eternity* on the wireless: 'I don't know what he said, but I knew it was clever.' Then he took us to his studio, where he brought out a guitar and sang Provençal love-songs. His eyes became wilder and wilder, sweat poured down his neck, and his toes were splayed out like claws. On the walls of the studio were a number of garish portraits in primary colours, the central feature of each being a single, huge, yellow eye. I think we all realized simultaneously that those eyes were none other than *Franzie's*. We were wondering whether to slip quietly away, when he suddenly stopped playing. He had seen us looking at the pictures, which he said had been done by his wife, an invalid. We were forced to go to a nearby convent to see this woman. It was clear that she was slowly dying. She sat bolt upright in a wheel-chair, her face bloodless and a mass of tiny wrinkles. As we stood looking at her, Franzie explained in her presence that she was paralysed and almost past speech. She might indeed have already been dead, except – again – for her eyes, which were full of peace and possessed a supernatural, faraway happiness. We heard later that Franzie was so poor that he was reduced to selling not only his own shoes, but his wife's.

Capri is a wonderful place for getting inhibitions out of your system. If you've always longed to wear a top hat with a bathing suit, or earrings down to your knees, or green powder, or gold ballet tights, nobody will stop you – or, probably, even stare. I rather fancied the Portuguese lady with cerulean lipstick, and with toenails and fingernails to match. Everyone has plenty of malicious stories about the goings on of everyone else, but the thing to do on hearing these is to adopt an air of vaguely amused cynicism.

A grizzly old *contadino*, who certainly did look a rogue, was pointed out to me as the father of twenty-six children by two women, both of whom lived in the same house. Then there was the beady-eyed V— reputed to have pushed a 'suicide' over the Migliara.

One of our visits was to the Signora Piumelli del Sasso, who lived in a cool shuttered house overlooking the Quisisana Hotel. The universal description of her seemed to be *simpaticissima*, and there was no doubt that she had once been very good-looking in a dusky Burne-Jonesy way. We found her languidly stretched out on a divan, heaped with brocade cushions, while cross-legged on the floor beside her were no less than three bald-headed swains in blue sailcloth trousers and sandals, revealing bare black-tufted toes. She offered to play the spinet to us, but we felt *de trop* and only stayed about twenty minutes.

Last night Elsa and Alberto took us to see the full moon rise from the top of the Phoenician steps near San Michele. Below us were the lights of Capri, and from Posillipo to Torre Annunziata the bay was picked out in yellow diamonds. Then came the moon, floating up from behind the mountains. The sea caught its reflection, and in the glittering trail across the water we saw the Sirens' rocks. . . .

Later. – I have just come back from a dinner party given by Aimée Randolph at the Bentrovata, a restaurant done up in Tyrolean style near Massalubrense, with hearts cut out in the shutters. It has such food, and such a view of Capri, that I am surprised it is not famous throughout the world. We had figs with raw ham this time, then veal *escalopes* with anchovy butter, followed by a marsala *zabaglione*.

The much coveted Beryl joined us. I talked so much about Anacapri that she started to call me Ana. The others copied her, and I was cross.

The Fifth Army have taken Viterbo. I wonder if Simon and Co. were involved, or if they were taken out of the line after Anzio. Stiffer resistance in Normandy. . . .

Tomorrow is the day I dread: my return to Naples. Gerard and Julian leave Sorrento too, and will be on the same boat.

11th June. Tamara

I had my stitches out at the 186th and spent last night there. Almost the first person I met was Ronnie, looking more like a bleached skull on a totem pole than ever. He told me we were not on speaking terms, so that was that.

I managed to keep my nerve right until the moment that we drove through the hospital gates. But when I saw the courtyard and that dark veranda outside the Clearance Ward, it was like an arctic wind rushing round inside me, and I knew I didn't even want to see *her* again.

The Sister in charge of the ward where I was to sleep had a face like an alcoholic Peter Pan's. I'm sure she hoped that her friends would describe her as elfish or mischievous. In reality she was nothing more than a raddled old wasp with a sting like an assegai. When I gave her my name, she cocked an eyebrow, and said: '*Christ*, not *the* R. Trevelyan? The Anzio Abelard?' And so I learnt that the whole hospital was 'mad' to see me, that 'people talked of nothing else', and that Celia had been transferred to Rome.

I wondered whether to hit the woman, really hard. My first reaction, though, was to freeze, and in those few seconds I had time to decide that the best way to disappoint her was to show absolutely no concern whatsoever.

Celia would never have made fun of me to other people. I wanted so much to be reassured. I even thought of hitch-hiking to Rome and returning in time for the Sorrento boat the next day.

169

It could have been Ronnie, but he had disappeared. . . .

I cut lunch at the hospital and spent the earlier part of the afternoon mooching round the officers' shop, buying shoes and pyjamas. Afterwards I went into an army information room in the Galleria, where they have maps with flags showing developments on all the fronts. The only other person in there was a Jewish-looking French major in glasses. I began to notice that, whenever I moved on to a different map, he would come too, standing so close that our shoulders touched. He smelt of garlic.

This game became boring. I strolled out into the Galleria and was soon conscious that he was following. The bars were beginning to fill up, so I slipped into one of the most crowded. There was an American top-sergeant alone at a table with a vacant chair, so I asked if I could join him.

The major appeared at the entrance. He had taken off his glasses, I suppose to make himself more attractive. For a few seconds he blinked round myopically, then took fright at the jabbering semi-drunken crowd, and went.

The American was called Fred and came from Wyoming. He would be thirty-four on 23rd June, he told me, and had been married for five years to a woman called Louise, whose photograph I saw. Evidently Louise was in a bad way; the doctor had forbidden her to have any children, she had recently had to have all her teeth out on account of 'gumrot', and peas and beans made her come out in lumps. Fred worked in the transport section of the P.B.S. (Peninsular Base Section). We talked a good deal about Capri and Algiers, but he was so ingenuous that I felt old and wicked and European.

The transport office had their evening meal at the unusual hour of four-thirty, so that the boys could 'hit the town' afterwards. Fred invited me to come to this meal with him, and then to a cinema show in camp – presumably laid on for those to whom hitting the town held no attractions. I accepted, and on arrival was issued with two tin plates, a mug, and a knife, fork and spoon. The dining-hall was shared by officers and sergeants, but whereas officers were waited on by civilian orderlies, the sergeants and I had to queue up for our fried chicken and coffee.

The film was a Western and excessively tedious – dozens of gun duels in saloon bars, and blondes being galloped away with. Fred suggested, when we came out, that we should visit some Italian friends of his; he said it was just about their *pasta* time. Ungratefully, I felt I couldn't face that drawl a moment longer – so, after an exchange of addresses in Wyoming and Essex, I left him and made for the Colorado.

Teresa was not there. I fell in with a sultry creature named Mici, who reminded me of Eustachia in *The Return of the Native*; you could imagine her walking under gorse bushes for the pleasure it gave her to feel the branches scratching against her hair. It was very hot, and after about a quarter of an hour I went upstairs for a breather – in any case, I wanted to shake off Mici, so that I could have the chance of sitting alone with a drink. As soon as I set foot inside the club again, I was seized by a furious little brown bundle of loose skin and matchsticks, dressed in black satin. I knew she was the *Madame*, but she screeched so that I couldn't understand a word. Then she pointed dramatically across the floor, and I saw Teresa, glowering at me from one of the chairs reserved for dance hostesses. An interested waiter offered to explain. Last week I had promised to come back to Teresa; why had I danced with Mici? Simply because Teresa wasn't there when I arrived, I replied. But I could have asked the *Madame* where she was; Teresa loved me, and wanted me to come home for love, not money. Two more waiters joined the group and started to titter. Suddenly everything went red, and I had one of my rare flare-ups. I sent the *Madame*, who had been clinging to my elbow all this time, spinning for a six, and snapped out that I had no intention of going home with Teresa for love or anything else. At that moment Mici appeared out of the Ladies and sauntered across the room towards us. Teresa at once leapt up and grabbed a fistful of the unsuspecting woman's hair. In a moment both were rolling on the floor. Flowers and pieces of jewellery flew in every direction. The band stopped playing, and some French officers cheered. I was left standing alone in the doorway, and so, ignominiously, made my escape. . . .

12th June. Tamara

I borrowed one of the Tamara boats this afternoon, and whilst rowing past the Tritone saw Silvia, with Lidia, another of the Croce daughters, and a young man standing on the jetty. All looked a trifle awkward and unhappy, so – as Silvia has become much less shy – I asked them to join me. The girls, who were wearing bathing suits, accepted at once, but the young man was in his best clothes and had to be left behind. I asked who he was, and Silvia casually replied that he was a Sicilian poet who had travelled up specially to see their father; as Benedetto Croce was too busy even to see the unfortunate fellow, Silvia and Lidia had been told to entertain him. Dismayed, I asked whether it was all right their coming out with me like this. 'Oh, yes,' said Silvia, yawning. 'If we stayed behind, we'd only have to listen to a five-thousand line poem about Daphnis and Chloë.'

I was asked to tea at the Tritone, and by that time the Sicilian poet had had to go back to Naples in order to catch his train to Palermo. Two other people had been invited, an American colonel and someone introduced to me as David, dressed in shorts and a scruffy khaki shirt without badges of rank. David appeared completely at home with the Croces, and at first, because of his moustache, I took him to be in the R.A.F., but later – for some unaccountable reason – to be a South African. Subsequently he turned out to be a Grenadier subaltern, recovering at the Palace from a bullet wound in the ankle. He told me that there is a civilian vegetable boat leaving at 8 a.m. tomorrow for Capri, so we have arranged to go there for the day. The American colonel remarked to Elena: 'It sure is strange how one song put that little old island on the map.'

I took Silvia and Lidia to their first cinema. It was a Betty Grable film, an appropriate initiation for Croces.

15th June. Tamara

Now Kip Manchester has been killed. At Retford we commanded a platoon together, and at Philippeville we shared a tent for two months. Kip, who by his example so often shamed me when I felt grudging or uncharitable about other people's efforts, who wanted so badly to take a 'real' part in this blasted war. . . .

He had parked his vehicle in an olive grove, not realizing that they were on the edge of a minefield. Then he went up, but was only wounded, with a piece in his spine. They thought he would pull through, and until the second night he was cheerful and making his usual jokes – when, quite suddenly, he was dead.

The letter telling me of Kip's death was waiting at the Tamara on my return from taking the Croces to the cinema. It was only handed to me very late in the evening, and by that time the telephone exchange had closed down. I wanted to call off the Capri trip, but had no alternative except to keep my appointment with David at the quay the next morning.

Immediately I saw David I told him that a friend had been killed. Instead of showing sympathy, he was almost brutally offhand. 'Good Lord,' he said, 'I expect friends of mine are being bumped off every twenty-four hours.' He turned away and made for the gangplank on to the boat.

It was no use telling him that Kip had been one of the best friends I'd had. Like the Tank Corps lieutenant at the C.C.S., he was just not that sort of person. If I had refused to go to Capri, the whole trip would have been spoilt for him.

And then I knew that if it had been I who had been killed, I would not have expected Kip to stay behind. So I never again mentioned the subject to David.

In point of fact we enjoyed Capri so much that we played truant from the Convalescent Home and spent two nights there. As usual, nobody seemed to pay the least attention to what was going on in the war. Now David and I are under a cloud and the Commandant says she has reported us as 'missing', which seems to be playing the school ma'am rather too hard. Despite the fact that she chose to call me 'you little fool, Ana', I was not as rude as David appears to have been when he went in separately to see her. We are to be reported to the District Medical officer, who comes over from Pompeii tomorrow.

I happen to know that this same D.M.O. is the boy-friend of Kitty Sandown, the one who met me with doughnuts as I came off the Anzio hospital ship; she also visited me at the 186th and sent reports home to Mother. I have hurriedly written to ask her to put on a special Delilah act on our behalf.

The real reason for our staying on at Capri was a

174

chance encounter in a bar at the top of the funicular. David and I were thirsty; we knew that Army regulations forbade the drinking of fresh water with fruit juice, but at the same time we didn't want any of that fizzy stuff. We were trying, in pidgin Italian, to explain to the barman that all we needed was the plain juice of oranges *without* water, when a tiny voice, seeming almost to come from under the counter, asked if she could interpret for us. And this was Mafalda; she was so small that our first impression was of nothing but a pair of dark glasses, like lemur's eyes, over a hibiscus-scarlet mouth. As David said afterwards, when describing her to somebody else: 'If you saw her shorts hanging on a clothes-line you'd think they belonged to a child of four.' In no time we found ourselves being called darlings, and had an invitation to a party at her villa that evening.

We couldn't possibly refuse. I telephoned the Faiellas to persuade them to put us up, and we each bought a natty Capri shirt and a pair of blue trousers *à la* del Sasso's admirers. I knew Aimée Randolph wouldn't mind and the Palace is so vast that, as David said (it turned out mistakenly), nobody would notice if you were away for a night or two.

Signora Faiella was making soap from the oil of her own olives. The Commendatore was all worked up about a cactus which he had creeping over one side of the villa. It came from Hawaii and flowered once a year for four hours before midnight, and he was expecting it to come out that evening or the next. Francis Brett Young had a cutting in England; the Commendatore gave me one too, and we wrapped it in cotton-wool so that I could send it home for planting in our greenhouse.

David (whose surname is Lemoye) turned out to be an exacting companion. He talked non-stop the whole time we were together, generally about the plots of novels or stories he had in mind to write. He also liked to see how far he could go without shocking me. 'You Wykehamists are so conventional,' he kept saying. Once, when we were walking up from bathing at the Marina Piccola, I took my sandals off and carried them on my head. David said that his opinion of me went up twenty per cent after that.

Then, again, I could never entirely believe anything that he told me about himself. It was always possible that he was 'testing' my gullibility. Every new topic would be prefaced with some such remark as: 'When I was packing citrus fruit in Casablanca,' 'When I was emptying lavatories in Winchelsea,' 'When I was a valet near the Marble Arch and wore my hair in a page-boy bob.' A favourite opening gambit would be: 'When I was on a ranch in California' – and I really do believe that he did once go to California. He also says he is an hereditary count of the Holy Roman Empire, and insists on being introduced everywhere as Count Lemoye. I have since found out that this claim of his is no lie either, and what's more, Queen Victoria gave his family a special licence to keep on the title – all of which makes him even more of a disconcerting character.

At the Faiellas' we were cornered by a Signora Preborio, bulbous and hirsute in the wrong places, with black brilliantined hair. She was learning English and begged us to take her on a walk. David cruelly suggested that we should make an expedition to the Lighthouse – a very dusty and difficult path – immediately after lunch during the heat of the afternoon. But nothing daunted, she came, and clambered along after us, streaming like a coal-heaver, chattering gaily away the whole time. At the Lighthouse David said he was going to bathe with nothing on, and even he was taken aback when she only roared with laughter and said she would enjoy watching him.

I shall always remember that party of Mafalda's because – let's face it – it was the first really adult party I'd ever been to. Hitherto the heights of sophistication for me had been to watch débutantes in tulle curtsying to a cake at Queen Charlotte's. Now I was hobnobbing on easy terms with all sorts of much-married *contesse* and White Russians of disreputable interests, not to mention a couple of American generals. Mafalda was in her most bubbling over of moods, and dragged me round after her, throwing her arms round this or that person and introducing me as 'this new *adorable* boy'. In between whiles she threw me snatches of information about herself: (*a*) she had no sense of smell; (*b*) she was married, and had to leave her children in Stockholm in 1940; (*c*) she had a grandmother whom she *adored*. Everywhere we went in the room we were shadowed by a swarthy captain of the American military police, hair *en brosse* and obviously much in love with her. She told me she detested him, but had to invite him to the occasional party as otherwise he would take away her permit to remain on Capri.

One of the most vivacious of the *contesse* was immensely struck by David, and invited us to come to another party at her house the following evening. That, said David, gave us a perfectly valid excuse for staying yet a further night on the island.

The next morning, we bathed from the Marina Piccola, near Gracie Fields' villa, now a club for American officers. Whilst we were lying on the raft, a girl swam out and clambered up beside us. She was so brown she might have been an Indian, and like all Italian girls did not wear a bathing-cap, so that her hair lay in long dark snakes down her back. 'Look, a mermaid,' David said to me. She laughed, and we discovered that she spoke English and that her name was Ivana. David wanted her to come to lunch, but she said she must ask Mamma first. We all swam to the shore together, where we discovered that

177

Mamma was none other than David's *contessa* from Mafalda's party. Ivana came to lunch with us, but – not surprisingly, perhaps – we were told that the evening's party had been cancelled.

I took David to see both Franzie and la del Sasso. We also went to the Faraglioni, for the sake of a laugh at the lovelies in their leopard-skin bathing suits, lounging about on rocks in carefully contrived attitudes.

Beyond the Faraglioni, and quite ruining that part of the coast, which would otherwise be completely wild, is the villa of Curzio Malaparte, author of *Kaput*. David had met him in Naples, so we went to pay a call. The villa is flat-roofed, roughly oblong in shape and painted orangy-red, like the colour of a *Casa di Cantoniera*; it is built on a jutting-out piece of rock so that when inside you feel as if you are in a ship. The sides of the fireplaces are of glass, giving an odd impression, for you are actually able to see the sea swirling beneath. Malaparte turned out to be away, and we were shown round by the housekeeper, with a pet lamb in attendance.

The climax of our stay was the flowering of the Commendatore's cactus. It was literally possible to see the petals uncurl; part pasque-flower, part lotus, part mandrake, it seemed to glow with a phantom brilliance through the night air. The scent, too, was so intense that it reached you fifty yards away.

16th June. Tamara

A touching, if pompous, letter has come from Julian. His last sentence is typical: 'Read a little, write a little every day.' I feel a brute for having quarrelled with him so often.

David and I were in due course hauled up in front of the D.M.O. I saw him first, and found that my appeal to

Kitty had done the trick. I was only given a mild rap, ending with an invitation to a drink with Kitty herself, who was coming to Sorrento in the afternoon.

When David came out, he looked sullen. I asked him what was wrong. 'The clot asked me why I saluted without a hat on. I told him we always did that in my regiment.' He is therefore to be returned to his battalion tomorrow. For my part, my time is up in any case; I leave on the 18th.

The Croces tell me that they asked David to do an article for their father's literary weekly, *La Critica*. He chose to write about the meaning of the word bogus.

I walked back to the Tamara in the dark, with only the crickets and fireflies for company. The olive trees against the sky made me think of a Chinese painting. It was so black and silent along there, that suddenly I felt overcome and for a long time was unable to continue either forwards or backwards.

18th June. Aversa

I am on my way now to the I.R.T.D., the Infantry Reinforcements Training Depot, the depot for lost souls. I sleep tonight in this dusty transit camp under canvas. Bully rissoles for supper.

THE RETURN

21st June, Sant' Agata dei Goti

PRITCHARD, my new batman, and I have just finished building a shelter of chestnut branches. A magpie clatters past. Swifts dive and swoop, as if the whole valley below were filled with the chutes of an aerial fairground.

The reason for my being here is that I am umpire on a Scheme. To be treated as a war-scarred veteran is all very well, but it's a bit thick being made use of like this so soon after my arrival at the I.R.T.D. We sleep tonight and tomorrow night in the open; I've almost got out of the way of it. At least I have been able to bring pyjamas – despite the fact that, ominously, the Scheme has been given the name Insomnia.

Now the bell in the campanile strikes six. We hear the voices of children, bathing in the green pond below the cliff on which the village is built. Every spare inch of this valley has been cultivated; the scene is a regular Joseph's coat of vines, maize, wheat, and terraced olives.

Clouds shift on the peaks opposite. Earlier today, the sun sent down two oblique rays, each illuminating for a few minutes one of the castles that, in this part of the world, are perched on all the most romantic and inaccessible points of vantage.

St. Agatha of the Goths; who was she, I wonder? Same old story no doubt – Blonde Christian Spurns Barbarian General.

This is also said to be the scene of the Caudine Forks, that arch-classic among unlikely place-names. Being thus reminded of Mr. Livy should, if anything, turn me against the valley. But it is such a tranquil place that even he, by association, has a sort of rosy halo at the moment. . . .

Toumi was waiting for me at the I.R.T.D. So were Gerard and Julian, and – to my surprise – Mepacrine. Our Anzio Battalion was taken out of the line three weeks ago, and is already on its way to the Middle East. Simon has gone too.

The first morning Toumi said we must take sandwiches into the woods above the camp. He led me to a half-ruined chapel, empty except for a worm-eaten crucifix and a cracked saint's skull in a box. Whilst we were standing in the doorway, a child's voice began to call shrilly from the undergrowth: 'TIMMI, TIMMI.' And, from all round us, like the highest notes of flutes, other voices echoed in reply: 'TIMMI, TIMMI, TIMMI.' In a moment we were surrounded by nearly a dozen ragged children, aged between five and seven, all barefoot and with tangled black hair and darting animal eyes. Toumi said they were his 'Wild Children'. He often came to share his sandwiches with them here. One, called Antonietta, had a piglet tied to a piece of twine. Another, Vito, had been picking wild strawberries.

They skipped about, pinching and chasing one another, and tweaking our uniforms. Everyone had to contribute to a pool of two-*lire* notes, and then Berto, whose behind showed through his tattered shorts, was sent down to the village to buy cherries and nougat. It was almost impossible to understand their dialect. Angelo's brother, we gathered, had found a job with the Allies at Foggia. News had just come through that Maria's father was a prisoner in America. A soldier had given Peppino an Egyptian piastre.

On Easter Day the children had made Toumi join a pilgrimage to a monastery, eight hundred feet up in the mountains. He had had to set out at dawn, and was the only non-Italian to attend the mass. An open-air breakfast followed: sugar cakes, *vino*, and the not very polite parts of a ram. Then the Madonna della Stella was carried down in procession to the village with Toumi following in the midst of a chanting throng of black-garbed peasants. He tried to look especially fervent, he told me, as he passed the I.R.T.D.

Toumi has a wonderful way with children. At La Peérouse one admirer, scarcely past the toddling stage, presented him with an egg just as we were setting off on a ten-mile route march. The shoeshine boys in Algiers always used to fight to clean his shoes. It was they who first called him 'Toumi', their version of Timmy, which is his real name.

Then there was the time at Philippeville, when we were sent on a snipers' course – Kip was with us. We used to have to wriggle about on our tummies in the scrub of the Djerbia Messouiene, but our positions were always given away by two little goatherds called Alouet and Hussein. The only words they knew in English were 'no damn good'. Their goats were 'no damn good', and we kept on being urged to snipe at them.

In the early mornings, sometimes before light, Alouet and Hussein used to bring eggs to our camp in the mandarine groves of Saint Antoine outside Philippeville. Those days seem an eternity from here. We used to fill our canvas buckets with mandarines (despite the notices *Attention! Pièges aux Hommes!*) and just gorge ourselves. Sometimes we went on night compass marches, and would visit the fly-blown kitchens of French settlers, under the pretext of asking for a glass of water, but knowing well that we would be plied with their vinegary white wine. . . .

Yesterday we hitch-hiked into Naples and visited another of Toumi's haunts: a restaurant called Guiseppone a Mare at Posillipo. We ordered lobsters, then went for a bathe.

We had swum out about thirty yards, when there were shouts from the shore and two chocolate-coloured figures dived into the water and trudgeoned strongly towards us. These were sisters, Renata and Vincenzina, again staunch friends of Toumi's. They had the almond eyes and straight noses of ancient Etruscans, and in their hair were pink oleander flowers. I noticed later that they had masses of black cat's fur under their arms; why will Italian women never shave?

Renata and Vincenzina loved swimming underwater. We had to dive down under the yachts and do 'ballets'. Afterwards we sat in the shade of an upturned boat and they sang 'Lili Marlene' in German. Toumi was amused by the way they made no secret of their admiration for the Germans, but I couldn't help feeling prudish. The waiter at Guiseppone's said that a German officer and his sergeant often used to go to lunch there too. *'Ufficial',* *tedesch' molto simile Lei,'* the waiter said to Toumi, and with gestures indicated that they had the same rather wavy hair and pointed chin.

Not far from Guiseppone's is Prince Umberto's house, guarded by gazelle-eyed *carabinieri* in tricorne hats. Farther along is Jumbo Wilson's villa, the Riv'Alta; then comes Harold Macmillan's.

Later we went to an open air night-club, the Orange Grove, in order to watch night fall over Naples. From there you have the famous view that appears in all nine-teenth-century books on Italy: an umbrella pine in the foreground, Castello dell'Ovo and Santa Lucia, and in the distance the curve of the bay to Vesuvius. The only thing nowadays that is lacking from the view is a couple of peasants dancing the tarantella.

French troops fighting in Elba. Thirty thousand Germans cut off at Cherbourg.

22nd June. Sant'Agata

8 a.m. In the early morning coolness of this Italian summer I was awoken by the sound of singing and of metal chiming against stone. Peasants are rebuilding the bridge, blown up by the Germans. Backwards and forwards, tirelessly, the strapping women go, with huge baskets of boulders on their heads; all the time they keep up a quavering half-oriental lilt.

Other Russell Flint ladies are working with sickles in a nearby field. They never straighten their backs to rest. Ceres, you feel, must be a bit of a slave-driver in these parts.

Now, as I write, three of our men come up the hill from the village. They have been in search of eggs – the eternal quest. It seems they have been successful, which augurs well for breakfast. People begin to wander up to the cook-house fire. As though attracted by the first whiffs of frying bacon, a group of Bisto Kids has suddenly appeared, squatting on the perimeter of the camp, and clutching tins with handles, like minnow-jars, in readiness for scraps.

The pleasantest part of this Scheme is its timelessness, a lack of the need to hurry. We came back late to camp last night and a brew was prepared for us. Then someone produced potatoes which we roasted in the embers, like good old Wolf Cub days. We sat talking for hours, allow-ing ourselves to become thoroughly sentimental, and it was two o'clock when I went to bed.

Near here I have discovered a quiet pool, with zigzag shadows and tall reeds with fluffy heads like pampas grass. It is just the place for Monty's hamadryads. For a good hour yesterday I sunbathed on a low rock. A violet and black dragonfly settled on me, and I saw a watersnake with an orange-crested head.

25th June. I.R.T.D., Rotondi

The days slip by. Perhaps tomorrow, perhaps next week, perhaps in two weeks' time, old Dame Fate will suddenly take it into her head to remember us, and will send each one hurtling off in the most unexpected direction. Meanwhile life is pleasantly idle, and we pay frequent visits to Naples.

This section of the I.R.T.D. is run by the Guards, and we are here very much on sufferance. Whether or not David was right in saying that his regiment saluted without hats, I have discovered that in the Coldstream it is practically *de rigueur* to wear your hat at breakfast. The colour sergeant is a real martinet, more of a puppet than a man. Gossip says that at home his family have to form up in pairs to march to church. He also has been known to salute the telephone after speaking to the Commanding Officer.

Julian is finding us much too frivolous and young. He has tried to persuade everyone in turn to come and read Dante in the woods, but without any success.

It is the fashion to hate Rotondi and the string of villages all along this road, more or less running into one another: Paolisi, Cervinara, Salamoni, Pirozza. People are irritated by the narrow leaning streets which make it difficult for a three-tonner to manoeuvre the corners, by the grimy babies piddling in public, by the W IL DUCES scrawled on the walls and the hostile looks from loungers outside the bead curtains on the *trattorie*. But who would not be hostile when every third house in your village is requisitioned, and Army trucks and carriers are churning up your orchards? I am happy among these bare-topped sugar-loaf hills, rising up above the chestnut woods where we meet Toumi's Wild Children. I love to hear the clopping in the streets before reveillé, and the women chanting as they set out for firewood. The mind is its own place.

Typical conversation overheard in the back of a truck when hitch-hiking to Naples:

'Hell, look at that. If there were a tank on that road, we could blow it to blazes from here.'

'Filthy country. Reminds me of Salisbury Plain.'

It is only too true that when we first arrived at the I.R.T.D. from Africa in February, these villages were a grim introduction to Italy, far from what we had expected. The ceaseless rain leaked on to our beds through the canvas roofs, and the only heat was from a small oil stove in the mess. Once when we were at lunch, an old woman broke into the dining-room and snatched some chop bones off my plate. Gun flashes lit up the night sky, and lorries were for ever rumbling northwards to the Front over the cobbles. Now that the sun is here, everything is changed. Mud-browns have become dancing yellows and greens; grey walls have turned white or a brilliant speedwell blue; and the peasants seem to have absorbed fresh energy from the warmth.

We have been again to Guiseppone's, this time with Mepacrine, who managed to scrounge a jeep from somewhere. Two F.A.N.Y. friends of Toumi's joined us. There was no sign of Renata and Vincenzina – no doubt they were being tactful, since we had female company. After lunch the girls decorated the jeep with bougainvillaea and oleander flowers, and we drove in a wild bacchanalian way to Pozzuoli and thence to the Solfatara, where the Martian landscape with its vaporous fumes and bubbling mire-holes had the effect of sobering us considerably. We dined at the Club, and later went up to the Orange Grove, to find it was already after closing time. Deirdre, one of the F.A.N.Y.s, produced two glasses of gin fizz. They had come from a deserted table, and she insisted that she had seen the owners leaving just as we arrived. Since we were thirsty, we all started taking swigs, only to be set upon immediately by a furious Beds and Herts captain and his Wren partner, returning from the dance floor. Five humiliating minutes followed, and we were only saved by a couple of boozy majors, whom I had met rather vaguely at Anzio, and who also appeared to be on familiar terms with the Wren. These majors told us that they were in charge of all the vehicles left behind by my ex-Division, now *en route* for the Middle East. 'You types short of transport?' they trumpeted. 'Come along tomorrow, all of you, to our depot at Capua' (they pronounced it Ker-pooah). 'We've bags of it. Three-tonners, carriers, jeeps, staff cars, you can take your pick.'

I meant to keep them to their word – the prospect of no more hitch-hiking or cadging lifts home seemed too good to be true. So the next morning I set out for Capua, taking with me Oliver Brace, who had been a racing motorist before the war and could therefore be relied upon to select the most roadworthy staff car (for I had determined it should be that). My two majors, however, were suffering from hangovers and in the stark light of day were in quite a different mood. It needed many highly coloured reminders of the Fortress and the Moletta Crossing before they could be persuaded to relinquish a pair of frumpy-looking fifteen hundredweights. Not being one of the world's most adept drivers, I have never fully mastered the art of double de-clutching, and so I would almost rather not have taken on my truck at all. But Oliver set off so precipitately that there was no time for havering.

I left with much grinding of gears. It was a job to keep up with Oliver. Then, on the road down into Naples from Aversa, the worst happened: my engine stopped. An obliging motor cyclist came to my rescue, but it meant having to navigate the Via Roma on my own, without Oliver in front of me as guide. What with the speed of the traffic, American military police whistling at me and *bambini* nipping in and out under my wheels, I don't think I've ever had such a scalp-searing experience.

The possession of Madam Fifteen Hundredweight, as Toumi calls her, is undoubtedly a boon. But neither he nor I have the faintest idea what to do if she collapses on us. . . .

Walking down the Via Roma yesterday evening Toumi and I felt suddenly consumed by hunger. We decided to accept the offer of egg and cheeps (in its literal sense, without trappings) from the next small boy who accosted us. He led us down the most Cimmerian of Off Limits alleys, bringing us out unexpectedly into a blaze of illuminations and activity. Here was a world into which we had never before penetrated. The lights came from rows of single-room houses, doors flung wide open to reveal every intimate detail of the interiors – beds, chamber-pots, kitchen utensils, statues of the Madonna. In front of each sat a monumental Momma, her black dress moulded to all the folds of her body generally with an infant or two crawling under her stool or scrabbling in a pile of refuse. The streets were jammed with people, everybody scolding one another, or shouting, or laughing, or singing. Carts rumbled, donkeys brayed, wirelesses poured out swing music, and in the wine-shops were real-life Neapolitan dagos strumming away at guitars.

When we reached our destination we found two privates of the R.A.S.C. already sitting at the table. They started up in alarm at the arrival of officers, and although we did our best to calm them, they remained quite speechless the whole time. We felt like badly disguised agents of the Fifth Column.

We had just finished our eggs, when the little boy rushed up, shouting: *'Polizia! Polizia!'* The privates bolted up a ladder into the loft, but Toumi insisted on staying where he was. It would be far worse, he said, if we were caught hiding.

The white-helmeted military police passed down the street in their jeep, but somehow managed to miss looking into the house where we were sitting.

26th June. Rotondi

We took Madam Fifteen Hundredweight to see Caserta Palace (now A.F.H.Q., Allied Forces Headquarters), and brought with us a picnic of sardine and cheese-spread sandwiches, plus a bottle of pink *spumante* and some peaches.

Madam gaily sailed through the main gates and was saluted from both sides. Not the least overawed, she then proceeded the whole length of the gardens, past ornamental pools and cascades, as far as the great 'basin', where people go to bathe and which is at the foot of the waterfall from Monte San Silvestro.

Here we disembarked, leaving Madam in the shade. In the middle of the basin are giant statues of Diana and her nymphs watching Actaeon being torn to bits by his hounds. You can be photographed sitting on one of these nymphs' knees (or in some other less elegant posture). One of the Americans, who was having his picture taken there, had soaped his hair, in order to make it look like marble, and had covered his body with white dusting powder.

After a bathe among the slightly nifty duck-weed, we went up to the grotto above the falls. Here we ate our picnic, and emboldened by the noise of tumbling water, sang arias from *Rigoletto*. Then home with Madam. . . .

At last my post is beginning to catch up. Aunt Jessie writes: 'And so you had five wounds, like the dear Lord.'

We occasionally have the tedious job of censoring letters. I found this today in Rifleman Hancock's letter:

> *I love you my Doris,*
> *My darling, my dear,*
> *Each moment I miss you*
> *And wish you were here.*
> *So remember my darling*
> *And please have no fear*
> *That soon I'll return*
> *And banish your tear.*
> *So good-bye my Doris,*
> *This poem I close,*
> *And with these short words*
> *My heart also goes.*

The end of the letter is not quite so poetical: 'Hoping this finds you darling as it leaves me. Cheerio darling and all the best darling from your loving sweetheart Alf. xxxx.'

I have discovered the meaning of Mizpah. It is Jacob's covenant with Laban: 'The Lord watch between me and thee, when we are absent one from another.'

27th June. Rotondi

The die is cast. The day after tomorrow we leave for the

Front, wherever that may be – somewhere near Perugia, I suppose. The advance is going so fast that it is difficult to catch up with the latest news. My twenty-first birthday is on the 6th; we now hope to celebrate it in Florence.

It is Jay's birthday on the 30th, his sixteenth. I have sent him a fine Sawdust Caesar dagger, with a shiny black sheath and a gold eagle's head as handle.

28th June. Rotondi

Just back from an *arrivederci* party in Naples. We had an enormous meal at the Andrea – *tagliatelle verdi*, lobster, wild strawberries, and white Chianti. Then up to the Orange Grove, where we sat on the balcony and for the last time watched the city light up. The band played 'As Time Goes By' for us.

30th June. By the Liri River

The sun is demoralizing. Here we lie on the Liri's bank – Toumi, Mepacrine, Oliver and I – soaking up the heat. We have been bathing with nothing on in the swift-flowing green water, much to the pretended disgust of some peasant women washing clothes. The vegetation crowds thickly and dustily to the river's edge, so that you think of Africa and the Elephant's Child. Then suddenly we come across spent schmeisser cases, not yet rusty.

The transit camp at Roccasecca is in a vineyard, now sheer desolation – just slit trenches and shell holes. The few remaining local inhabitants stare at us with a skulking hatred. We slept last night in the open air; when I woke up, both my eyelids were swollen from mosquito bites. This afternoon we move on to somewhere outside Rome.

We came up as far as here by rail. It amazed me that

they had got the trains running again so quickly. We passed through Cassino at nightfall, at that moment of dusk that I used to dread so much at Anzio. In the sepia light the crags of masonry might have been the ruined Alcazar of Toledo as painted by a modern Greco. Above us were the Monastery and Hangman's Hill. I had the feeling that the place was not empty, but *stifled*, as if the souls of all those thousands taken in sudden death had not yet had time to free themselves. People say that the ruins should be left as they are; what more appropriate memorial indeed could there be to this war, and to all wars?

The sight of burnt-out tanks, groundsheets trailing from sandbagged trenches, trees with naked branches like the roots of decayed teeth, graves marked by bayonets topped crazily with helmets, all these made me realize how – in a way unconsciously – I had been shutting out the memory of the past months. At Rotondi, when we had been told that, at last, we were going to be sent to one of the Regiment's battalions, we had been excited; our vanity was satisfied, and we would be meeting old friends again. But this glimpse of Cassino made me see everything in perspective. I lit a cigarette, then another from the stub; then another. It was the first time I had felt the need to smoke like that.

A few miles short of Cassino the train stopped for about an hour. We got out in search of eggs and water for a brew. It was like wandering on one of those huge levelled rubbish dumps at the mouth of the Thames. We could only find one inhabited farmhouse. There seemed to be about thirty people of all ages, from old crones to babies, living in the cellar. We saw at once it would be pure cruelty to demand eggs from them, even at a high price. What use could money be here? They seemed too wretched even to care about clearing away the mess of broken Army equipment and old tins scattered around their yard. And over all was the familiar stench of decay and unburied faeces.[1]

Later. – 6 p.m. Now we are camped in a field near the Appian Way. The vehicles have formed a 'lager' round the bivvy tents where we are to sleep. Indian corn, one of my passions, is growing in the next field. I picked some cobs, still greenish, and ate them raw.

9 p.m. There is an Ordnance dump down the way. I felt impelled to go there, to ask if they had a telephone. I had to hear Celia's voice before I reached the Front.

Although we cannot be more than ten miles from Rome, it was necessary to get through first to Freedom, the A.F.H.Q. exchange. I spent half an hour shouting down the field telephone and winding the handle. Then, at long last, her hospital answered me.

They said Celia was in. I knew she would never come if I gave my own name, so I said I was Captain Barnes – that R.E.M.E. captain.

Almost at once the line began to crackle. Then there was her voice, the same self-assured tones – and I could see her so clearly, just as she had been when she left me, twenty-six days ago in that library. I wished I had not gone so far as this, that I had not tried to telephone her at all, that time could somehow be blocked, or put into reverse. I was sure that the next moments could only hurt me.

But although I heard every word she said, the crackling

[1] Two years later, after the war, I was driving south to Naples on duty. My driver, Marocco, came from Cassino and I had agreed to drop him at his home. I discovered that it was his family living in this very house, which was still in exactly the same condition as that day in 1944; no attempt had been made to clear away the relics of battle, let alone rebuild the farm. Marocco said this was because they were still waiting for officials from Rome to come and assess the damage.

was so bad that she didn't even know it was really I who was telephoning her. After about a minute she hung up. . . .

10.30 p.m. For an hour I have been lying on my bed, thinking about those days at the 186th, and about Celia. Perhaps it was as well that I couldn't speak to her just now. Life at this moment should be as uncomplicated as possible. Or am I beginning to see things in perspective?

1st July. Terni

We are camped in an olive grove on a mountainside covered with rocks like crouching griffons and flop-eared dragons. The young trees barely give us shade, and the cicadas are scraping frantically away, the only living things stirred to energy by this heat.

We drove through the suburbs of Rome not long after first light. The streets were being washed. We managed to startle one very old tram, which went panicking away at great speed and with much clanking.

From Rome onwards, up the Via Flaminia to Narni and then to Terni, the troop carriers went bonnet to tail, sending up dense clouds of dust, so that we had to tie handkerchiefs over our noses. Everyone's face became a subhuman floured mask with red-rimmed eyes blinking out. 'So like a film,' said Toumi. 'Rather a long one, though.'

A Scots Guards captain has joined us at this camp. He has just flown from Cairo, via Valetta. We asked him what Malta was like. 'Jolly good stone wall country,' was his only comment.

Another transit camp, the most civilized yet. Discipline is less aggressive, as is always the case when you get nearer to the fighting. This is the last stop before the Front itself, and the battalion commanders come here to select reinforcements. We half expect them to go round pinching our biceps and tapping our front teeth, as if we were potential gladiators or reinforcements for the Legions.

The Camp Commandant is obviously a man of taste. He does his best to make the food more interesting, and we had *pasta* for lunch. The Blimps are up in arms, complaining that they are being forced to eat 'indigestible Wop muck'.

The cups and plates in the mess are local majolica – a lime-yellow and green design, with medieval figures like the knaves and queens on playing cards. The Commandant says you can buy majolica very cheaply in Orvieto, in fact one plate costs the equivalent of sixpence. I long to be able to go into the town by day and see the cathedral, but we are not allowed to do this in case there is a sudden call to the Front. Toumi and I did in fact manage to sneak in after blackout last night, by means of the Scots Guards captain's jeep. The streets were so dark that we might have been anywhere – driving along Kingsgate Street at Winchester, or Petergate at York.

We went afterwards to a small lake, not far from the camp. The water was so warm that we bathed for over half an hour. Toumi collected a lot of fireflies, which he put on a water lily leaf and waved about like a torch as he swam. In the middle of the lake was a miniature island, with the painted figure of a stork standing on it. We realized that we must be in the grounds of some large country house and decided to explore. Before very long we found ourselves near a group of buildings. Dogs barked and a terrified little man came rushing out, screaming at us and waving a shotgun. We felt it would be best to make off, if only to keep the peace. No doubt he is now congratulating himself on his presence of mind.

5th July. Near Cortona

And so tomorrow I come of age. Mother does not know I am back in the line. She will be thinking of me now, wondering how I shall be spending my birthday. We had planned once to have a dance at Sawkins [our house in Essex], and if the weather was fine enough, it was to have been on the terrace. Are the romneya nearly out? Mother always said they flowered on my birthday.

Instead, I write this in a clover field in Tuscany. Jazz throbs out from the wirelesses under the camouflage nets. Tanks creak on the other side of the hedge. Some of my men, stripped to the waist, are brewing the platoon char in a dixie. The Italian farmer stands at a distance, resigned.

Tomorrow we go forward to the outskirts of Arezzo, to protect the armour. Once more the supreme test is facing me. I have to keep reading and rereading the twenty-third Psalm. Just now shells were bursting on the hillside above Cortona. In between explosions we could hear the bells of the little ochre-coloured monastery, which seemed to be right in the centre of the firing.

In some ways today seems the most important in my life. I remember Father saying on embarkation leave that the worst part of battle was wondering beforehand how you were going to behave in front of other people. When I arrived at Anzio, war was like a game; I had no idea of the consequences of danger. I don't think even now I really fear death, or the process of dying. It is only the thought of whether or not I shall acquit myself honourably tomorrow that obsesses me.

About half a mile from here there is a bridge which is being bombarded by the Germans. We have grown tired of watching the puffs of dust, and hardly notice the continual clump-clumping any more.

Yet, somehow, despite all this, Tuscany has an air of peace and is full of quiet, gentle colours. The fields are wreathed with vines and dotted with the red pantiles of farmhouses. Cypresses are in all the most absurdly picturesque places. Lake Trasimene is behind us, placid and unrippled, except for a few fishermen's boats, caring nothing for the war. At seven o'clock this morning we passed along the edge of the lake. There was a heat haze, and at first all we could see were the reeds and a few boats tethered to poles. Then, suddenly, the mist lifted a little, and we saw a ghost island, an Avalon, with houses piled up round the campanile.

I arrived last night at the Battalion. After so much string-pulling, so many hopes and fears, it is nothing but an anti-climax. Only the senior officers are at all congenial; the others are inconceivably stuffy and grand — mostly made up from sergeants in the Desert, and therefore jealous of their status. I have also been fobbed off with the dregs of the Battalion for my platoon, one or two of the men being old sweats just out of the glasshouse.

Someone has come up to say that the Russians have taken Minsk and are advancing on Vilna. Normandy is going well. We all feel cheered, as if these successes far away can lighten even our most immediate prospects.

Later. – I am to go into the attack tonight. There has been a change of plan. I have been chosen to lead the Company attack because I am 'fresh'. Toumi knows how

I am feeling, and characteristically offered to take my place. He was told that it was an action which needed battle experience.

It seems that the advance on Arezzo is not turning out as we had hoped. Germans are still on the heights above San Sebastiano and are therefore commanding the vital Route 71. To drive them off these heights is to be our objective tonight.

PART THREE

Trasimene

NIGHTS ON THE BARE MOUNTAIN

Toumi had brought up the relief party with the extra water and the rations. His face looked blotchy under the toadstool-like tin hat with its hair-net (as he always called it) of camouflage netting.

Scree rattled down the mountainside. He dragged himself on all-fours into the trench beside me.

'Many happy returns,' he whispered. 'Here's the key of the door. The champagne from Fortnum's to follow.'

It was an enormous key, pinched, no doubt, from some barn belonging to the little farmer who owned the land above San Sebastiano, where we had assembled for the attack the previous evening. I felt uneasy having Toumi with me; he seemed to belong to a separate world, one that had no right to encroach on me in these circumstances.

Indigo shadows dwindled in the ravine far below. Toumi, without so much as pausing for an answer to his questions about what it felt like to be twenty-one, went into rhapsodies over the view of the Tuscan plain, with its distant *blick* of Lake Trasimene, just emerging into the full morning light.

There was no need to whisper, I told him. The nearest Germans were at least three hundred yards away. I took delight in pointing out where they had been firing, only a couple of hours previously.

He stayed about five minutes more. After he had gone I

was busy sorting out the rations with my sergeant. It was difficult to move from trench to trench; we were all convinced that the Germans were watching us, and that they were merely holding off their fire for some strange reason of their own.

The men were very glum. I had the impression that they blamed me for our predicament: stuck on a mountain top, with little more than badger-scrapings for cover, and blind to the only line of attack. Archie Bates, our Company Commander, had warned me that the men in my platoon were nothing but a bunch of odds and sods, even a few ex-deserters being among them. Until my arrival at the Battalion, they had been without an officer, and life must have been moderately peaceful. But now that I had come along – with three months' experience at Anzio – they had been sent into action immediately.

Toumi's offer to take my place in the attack must have made Archie think again, for in the end I was only put in charge of the second wave. Not that it was much of an attack in the orthodox manner of speaking. Little else was involved for my platoon than a stiff climb up a mountain under an aching load of weapons, picks and shovels. Our denims clammy with sweat, we hauled ourselves in single file along the valley up the side of the Maggiore. The moon was full, making the outlines of rocks stand out like strokes of crayons. Our own shells whistled comfortingly overhead and crumped down on the summit above. Occasionally a stray Jerry replied, and we were glad of a few seconds' enforced rest, when we had to fling ourselves down for cover in the resiny-smelling scrub. Then, some way in front, came urgent irritated bursts of automatic fire. The first wave had evidently run into the Jerry defences. But we had to keep on; up, up, gasping under our loads. At last, when we had climbed out of the valley, and the scrub had turned into loose stones and shale, we moved into extended order. The sudden silence ahead was baffling, until we came on one of the platoons of the first wave digging in. The enemy had withdrawn, we were told. At that moment Archie Bates' shape hulked out into the moonlight. I must dig in too, he said, over there on the right, covering that saddle.

Archie led the way to the ledge under the Maggiore's crest where we were to dig our trenches. He began to tell me what had been happening, how the sergeant of 16 Platoon had behaved magnificently, dashing alone into the Jerries' position – when suddenly crisis enveloped us. A spandau opened up from the opposite ridge, across the saddle. Like quick fluorescent bees the tracer darted over and pricked up the stones all round us. I could feel Archie's body panting against me as we lay flat on the stones; together we seemed such a large target, and I wanted to edge away from him. A few yards from us a man screamed, then moaned softly.

The firing petered out after a few minutes. There was about an hour and a half left before daybreak. We hacked frenziedly at the ground with our picks, but solid rock was only just below the surface and we had to rely on parapets of stones for protection. Sometimes the spandau would open up again, just a few short bursts at a time, as if to reassert its supremacy.

For the purpose of defence our position was against every conceivable rule. Completely isolated from the rest of the Company and no doubt in full view of the enemy during daylight, we were quite unable to deal with an attack until the Jerries were right on top of us. They could reach the crest, only ten yards away, and fire straight down on our heads, point-blank. There would have been little chance of retaliating.

It was when the first gleams of daylight were appearing on the horizon that I crawled over to the sergeant for an exchange of views. Almost simultaneously, like echoes of our fears, automatic fire started up on the other side of the crest. The counter-attack! We waited, watching the sky-line above, with our weapons cocked. We heard grenades; tommy-gun answered schmeisser; distant voices shouted indistinguishable commands. Then, quite suddenly again, silence – but only for a short while. From our own lines, down in the valley, came the D.F. barrage, shells screeching and thumping viciously on to the crest. They were falling much too close. Showers of stones and dirt pelted down on us after each explosion. Two men were crying out – it seemed as if their nerve had broken. The sergeant bellowed orders at the wireless operator.

By the time the barrage had stopped, it was broad daylight. In the silence we heard groans from the crest above. They could only have come from somebody in the greatest agony. We were taken aback by the sound, for we had not realized that anyone could have been quite so close to us. To crawl up there to investigate might mean considerable risk, with the possibility of snipers observing us from the other side of the saddle. I looked inquiringly at the sergeant, but he avoided my eyes. I realized that every other member of the platoon was deliberately turning away from me, in case I happened to pick on him. Meanwhile the groans continued. I had to decide. So I went myself.

A signaller was lying on his stomach in a half-dug trench. I turned him over and recognized Loftus 05 of 17 Platoon; he had been helping me with my kit when I first arrived at the Battalion. Thick crimson blood was welling out of a hole in his temple. He was gasping with great deep shudders. I tried to take off his helmet, but it was caught up with his wireless aerial. I didn't want his blood to touch my hands. The straps on his shoulders were difficult to unloose. If only I could get him free of the wireless, he might be able to breathe more easily. His eyes were glazed. I tried to say encouraging things, although I knew he could not hear me. I was still struggling with his straps when more shells came over from our lines. They exploded very close. Up there on the crest there was even less shelter than in my own trench. Loftus was still gasping, sometimes letting out small gurgles. He vomited and the blood was all over my denims. If I stayed there and managed to unbuckle his wireless would I ever be able to save his life? A shell burst quite close to us. I left Loftus and scrambled back down the slope to my platoon.

As soon as I saw the sergeant, I knew that I would have to lie to him. He looked at the blood on me, and said: 'Who was it?' I told him that it was Loftus 05 of 17 Platoon. 'Is he dead?' 'Yes.'

The shells had stopped falling almost as soon as I had reached my trench. There were no more groans from the crest. I prayed that Loftus would not betray me.

The sun began to climb in the cloudless July sky. We could see the terracotta roofs of the small town of Cortona, where Signorelli was born. Farther away, surrounded by fields the colour of dirty gold with patches of vegetable green, was Lake Trasimene. Trasimene, where another battle once took place – Hannibal. I thought of hours spent swotting for School Certificate. In two thousand years' time, perhaps, schoolboys would read about *this* war in 1944 and find it equally boring.

We drained the last water from our bottles. Until Toumi arrived with the rations, we had nothing to eat. And until he reminded me, I had quite forgotten that it was my twenty-first birthday.

We felt better after food. There was no sign of movement from the other side of the saddle. We took it in turns to watch with field glasses. Three tanks, like tortoises, moved up a winding dusty road in the ravine. Rumours reached us that the Indian Division was on the outskirts of Arezzo. The wireless operator had established good contact with Company Headquarters. He tuned in every ten minutes. 'Hallo Oboe 3, hallo Oboe 3, report my signals. Over.'

In the afternoon a code message came over the air for me to report to Archie Bates. We had long lost our fear of snipers from the other ridge, so I ran half-doubled up to Headquarters.

Archie's manner was curiously polite, and at the same time aloof. We had known each other at school and so it was more than ever absurd that he should now treat me as if I were some unwanted stranger at a formal tea-party. He began by asking me how I felt, and then went on to apologize for the position of my platoon. I was more or less in reserve, he explained, and so it didn't really matter if I had a restricted field of fire.

He then went on to say that it had been decided that we should spend another night on the Maggiore. The trouble was that the Indians had still not yet taken Arezzo, and until this happened, the Jerries were not likely to want to withdraw from these mountains overlooking Route 71.

'And this is where you come in,' he went on hurriedly. Spandau Ridge, as he called it, was still an unknown quantity. Before Divisional H.Q. could decide whether to push through another battalion on our right, they had to know whether Spandau Ridge was unoccupied or not. At 23.30 hours, therefore, a small patrol – consisting of myself and one or two other men – was to approach the Ridge and try to draw enemy fire. As soon as we succeeded in doing this, we were to return at once.

'But the country's completely open,' I blurted out. 'There's no cover at all. And there'll be a full moon.'

Archie started speaking very fast. He said something about moonlight being surprisingly deceptive; then about there being plenty of rocks and scrub around for cover, and, anyhow, it had to be done.

'We chose you because the other chaps are shagged out. They've already had to cope with the first attack *and* the counter-attack.'

It was an effort to concentrate on the rest of what Archie had to say. He gave me the details of warning signals if the company were attacked: a white Very light would mean that the Jerries had come in force; a red and a green Very light would mean that I must withdraw my platoon.

When I told the sergeant about the patrol, he was very indignant. 'Suicide squad!' he said so loudly that everybody in the next trenches overheard him. We decided that there would be less risk if I took only one man with me. The obvious choice was Davies, a tall lance-corporal who always wore a cap comforter under his helmet, 'the only reliable bloke in this shower,' as the sergeant said.

I found myself unable to think of home, or Celia, or my family, even to make plans with Davies about the line of approach that we would adopt. My feelings were numbed. Davies, on the other hand, was quite impassive, oiling his tommy-gun, priming grenades, studying Spandau Ridge through field-glasses. It was the sergeant who suggested that I should try to doze off. I was grateful to him, and immediately fell into a heavy dreamless sleep. He roused me at dusk for stand-to, and then insisted that I should continue sleeping until the time for my patrol.

Pandemonium woke me. Bullets, mostly tracer, were flying in all directions above our trenches. I could hear voices shouting both in English and German. The bursts of schmeisser seemed to be just on the other side of the crest.

The sergeant was doubling up and down the line of

trenches. 'Bloody death-trap,' he yelled at me. 'No wonder the men are bolshie.' Several grenades burst. The air was heavy with cordite. A voice, with a shrill note of panic, reached us out of the night. 'Look *out*, 18 Platoon. They're coming for you.' We crouched with tommy-guns covering the skyline, waiting.

Three Very lights went up: green, then red, then white. All the landscape, our faces and our weapons were garishly illuminated. Why three lights? And why in that order? There was a noise of boots scrambling over stones and scree, and in the last flicker of the Verys I saw half my men bolting down the mountain-side.

'Stop them,' I shouted to the sergeant. 'No use,' he shouted back. 'We've got to get out of here.' I stuffed as many grenades as I could into my trouser pockets. 'Right. Let's go. But keep together.'

I remembered too late that I had left my field-glasses behind. We stumbled over the rocks in our eagerness to get away from the crest. Two hundred yards or so down I called a halt. The bullets were no longer flying and there was complete silence, except for our breathing, on the mountain.

I told the sergeant to re-form the remnants of the platoon and to take up firing positions; meanwhile Davies and I would go forward and find out what was happening at Company H.Q. on the crest. At the back of my mind was a maxim from training days at York – *depth in defence*. Either Archie would be glad to use us as reinforcements, or else we would be there to cover his withdrawal, should this be necessary.

The moonlight had turned the rocks into great contorted bergs of silence, as we climbed the mountain-side again. Davies kept lagging behind, and I had to beckon to him to hurry. When it seemed as if we must be near the Company positions, I began calling out in a half-whisper:

'A Company, A Company. Are you there, A Company?'

The first trench I reached was empty. I called once again, straining to catch some sign of movement.

Down in the valley behind me, from our lines, a mortar fired. Within the space of a second the shell had come crashing down on the mountain, only a few dozen yards away from me, and sending up a vast fountain of sparks and fire. Shrapnel was spitting all round. Then came another shell, and another. A fourth landed, only just to my rear, a moment after I had thrown myself face down into the shallow trench. I was half-buried by stones and broken pieces of rock.

There were several more shells. I had absolutely forgotten about Davies. During a short lull I became aware of shouted commands and the cries of wounded men. The shouts were in German. It was then that I realized what had happened: the Company had withdrawn and their positions had been overrun, and now our own mortars were putting down a counter-barrage. The only thing I could do was to wait for a further lull in the shelling, and make a run for it.

The lull came. I jumped up and took my first step out of the trench, and the whole world cracked open in a sheet of flames. There was a noise like a dinner gong ringing inside my head. My face was all sticky and hot liquid streamed into my eyes. I knew that a shell had hit me, but I felt no pain. As I staggered downhill, my left arm felt numb and loose – I was quite unable to lift it when I tried to wipe my eyes.

I kept falling over rocks. As I moved dizzily on, the inside of my thighs began to sting; I realized I had been hit there too. I wanted to take the grenades out of my pockets in case more shrapnel exploded them, but I didn't dare stop for fear of fainting. Then my knee felt stiff, and when I hit it against a rock, it began to hurt. All the time I was remembering Loftus 05. If I collapsed on the mountain, there would be nobody to help me.

Silhouettes of trees wavered in the moonlight. That meant I was reaching the valley. I saw people moving. 'Stretcher-bearer,' I managed to call. Two men came up. They took off my helmet and wanted to put field-dressings on my head and arm. I refused to let them do this. Whenever I stopped moving, I began to lose consciousness.

They had not realized that I was an officer. I walked with my good arm round the neck of one of them. The other man held me round the waist. The trees grew bigger and blacker, shutting out the moon. We were nearly at Battalion H.Q.

In a pool of light I came face to face with Archie Bates.

It was difficult to speak. 'Hallo, Archie,' I said.

He peered close, trying to recognize me. Finally he said: 'Good God. I sent Toumi up there to fetch you back.'

Everything was swimming, slipping; high up on the Maggiore I could just hear the first bursts of automatic firing.

THE Maggiore was not finally secured until a day or two later. I was taken to a field hospital near Perugia, then flown to Naples.

On the night of 26th July Toumi was killed. He and some others had been sent on a patrol to occupy a farm, thought to have been already clear of enemy. Outside the buildings they had come face to face with a man; they had realized too late that he was a German.

By the end of the month I was back at the Villa Tamara. I stayed there until the middle of October.

RETURN TO ANZIO

January, 1969

WHEN I was a boy I had some friends who would climb on the dining-room table and make the electric light swing if their father started reminiscing about World War I. I thought of the poor father recently when, perfectly cool, feeling by no means square, I hired a Fiat 600 in Rome and set off for some sand-dunes about thirty miles to the south. On those dunes, on 23rd May, 1944, the Green Howards battalion to which I was attached lost 230 men – not all killed admittedly; some were wounded or taken prisoner. It had been the day of the breakout from the Anzio Beachhead.

As we batted along the Via Ostiense, in the Fiat, I kept telling myself that I wasn't ashamed of my journey. After all that day had always seemed a far more important anniversary to me than any other, including birthdays. What's more, it was easy to remember, as every year it coincides with the Chelsea Flower Show.

The place was still a horrible one in which to die, though barely recognizable. Our battalion had been carrying out a 'diversion' – innocuous word. An hour before dawn we had had to attack northwards across the Moletta River. There were no houses then, only one or two beach-huts, which I never saw.

Now that whole coast is a sprawl of gimcrack villas – all the more depressing because they are obviously the prized weekend havens of families of Roman businessmen. The Moletta smells and frogs plop up like ordure; the sand looks as though it is sprayed with coal-dust and is scattered with broken glass, plastic bottles, whitened tree trunks, old shoes and rusty sardine tins; the scrub, among which I imagined I could still make out the lines of German slit-trenches, belongs in reality to some blasted heath, where nasty old men might strangle girls with nylons.

I noted that on the very site where one of my best friends had been killed, with an anti-tank bullet in his face, there is a dancing-place called the Calypso. All I could think about was haunted rectories, and the hubbub feeble-minded people make about ghosts when they hear that an old soul has died alone in her bed in some such place a hundred years ago. What do the dancers at the Calypso feel about ghosts? Would they care if I told them about 23rd May 1944? I doubt it, and they would be quite right not to care.

One thing I was determined to do was to swim in the sea, however rough, cold and dirty, as close as possible to the mouth of that damned Moletta. There was quite a current, and as I struggled to keep my balance in the waves, I began to muse. I really let myself go with my musing, and rather enjoyed it. Courage, fear, *esprit de corps,* self-preservation, patriotism, youth, war as a substitute for violence, I mused on the whole lot....

In a way I had been idealistic and I had known vaguely what I was fighting for, yet strangely I had none of the fury against my opponents that twenty-year-old students today seem to feel against policemen. Indeed I never felt fury against any German while I was at Anzio. When I first went into the line early in March, to that part of the Beachhead where the trench warfare is supposed to have been the nearest thing during the last war to Mons or

Ypres in 1915, I did some reckless, idiot things and risked my life often and without need. I only did them out of inexperience.

War then really did seem a kind of game – a cliché, but true. Gradually, very gradually, my nerves became eroded, mainly because of the waiting. . . . To hear a wretch crying out in no-man's land and to be unable to help him was enough to age anyone ten years overnight.

Three days before the breakout, just a couple of hundred yards from where I was swimming, I had been leading a recce patrol and had taken the wrong turn. I was lucky. I didn't step on the *schu*-mine. But my corporal did, Lance-Corporal Atkinson, a silent, dark man with thick eyebrows and a sallow face. . . . He had trusted me and I had liked him too, but he was still alive. It was my fault. That was a real turning point for me. From that moment I knew I would not just be afraid in battle, but afraid of showing that I was afraid. I know now too, that I would still feel the same if ever I had to go again to the front as a platoon commander.

When at last we marched up to the attack I swallowed a Benzedrine that the M.O. had given me. Suddenly I felt marvellous. . . . Just then our signals man deliberately fired a bullet through his foot. I was shocked and furious. Cowardice! Yes, furious; that was one of the occasions when I really did feel fury.

Our mortar barrage lifted and we charged with fixed bayonets, towards the dazed Germans, towards the Calypso. Then I did another bloody stupid, terrible thing. Instead of plunging into the scrub and thus taking the German machine gun posts from the rear, in accordance with the basic rules drummed into me at O.C.T.U., I took a section of men along the outside perimeter.

A Spandau opened up. . . . I knew he had died. A funny red-cheeked fellow Corporal Peter had been; his feet had stunk so bad that one couldn't bear to be in the same trench with him. He too had trusted me. Everyone else in the section had been hit, either killed or badly wounded. . . .

I thought of all these things, things which I had nearly forgotten, among the waves at the mouth of the Moletta. It's quite a luxury to be maudlin cnce in a while. I brooded a bit on other matters, like youth having to bear the brunt of danger in wars. How smart of the old ones, I thought, to catch the fledglings before they have time to learn about anguish. I tried then to justify my own behaviour. Fancy expecting someone of twenty to have such responsibility, with decisions involving life and death. Ridiculous. God knows I had tried to redeem myself during the rest of that morning, while the effects of the Benzedrine lasted. I had in truth behaved like a savage animal. Fury once more; the second time that day.

Then came the reaction. One of our men lost his foot. . . . The memory of what I had done to Corporal Peter, Lance Corporal Atkinson and the others stayed raw and ragged on my conscience for years.

For lunch, I thought of the Calypso, but decided instead to go to the Paradiso, a big restaurant, faintly Tyrolean, built almost where Atkinson had been blown up. My companion and I ate the *specialità di casa*, huge devilled prawns, delicious, with *insalata verde* and *vino dei Castelli*. On an impulse I told the waiter that I had been on that very spot during the war and had nearly died there. I thought it might amuse him, but he made no comment.

I drove half a mile inland, to San Lorenzo where I had spent three weeks, under a cowshed. What had once been a hamlet is now a building estate called Nuova California. Masses of villas, grander than those round the Calypso and the Paradiso, are going up on a stretch of grassland that in my time had been a mine-field, covered with wild lupins.

My morbid mind got to work, and I remember the inflated bodies of white oxen, that had wandered on to the mines and had lain there for weeks, stinking under the Italian sun. I saw a butcher's shop at San Lorenzo with the sign *Macelleria – tutte le carne fresche.* Aha, I thought, very significant, very poetic; I must note that down. Then I caught sight of some words roughly painted on a gatepost at the beginning of what we used to call the Lateral Road: Via Campo di Carne.

The Campo di Carne was the ironically appropriate name for the open ground in front of the notorious Fly-over Bridge, near the even more ironically named Buon-riposo Ridge. There, between 16th and 20th February, the fate of the Beachhead had been in truth decided. The American 45th and 3rd Divisions, after the Royal Fusiliers and the Oxford and Bucks, and later the Loyals, had been overrun, had moved in and had only just managed to prevent, thanks to a colossal air bombardment, what easily might have been real and total disaster, even worse than Dunkirk. They had lost about 5,000 men in those four days, bringing their total casualties since the landings on 22nd January to 19,000.

Until then the British 1st and 56th Divisions had taken the toll on that battered, muddy, corpse-strewn land-scape. The Factory. Carroceto. Campoleone Railway Station. The Bowling Alley. The Embankment. Hundreds of British soldiers had died in those places – the exact casualty figures still are surprisingly difficult to get hold of. Now that I can sit comfortably in my armchair and read about what really happened, I can in some ways be thankful that I was only sent to the Beachhead on 1st March, when the 'lull' had started and there was no longer any fear of a major German counter-attack; when the front was regarded as static, and the deadly, gory toing and froing in miserable, teeming weather was to all intents over.

After 20th February Anzio, as a battlefield, came to mean something quite different. It turned into a much more personal war, more confined. Most of the fighting, in the British sector, took place in the deep, scrub-filled fissures. . . . Any battalion going to the Fortress would reckon on losing a third of its personnel within a week. There were other positions in the wadis almost equally dreaded: the Elbow, the Starfish, the Lobster's Claw, the Boot, the Culvert.

One hardly felt inclined, let alone was allowed, to go visiting or sightseeing. In fact during the three months I was at the Beachhead, I scarcely got to know anyone outside my own platoon. When we came out of the line for three or four days' rest in the *pineta* outside the town of Anzio, we only wanted to sleep.

I drove along the Via Campo di Carne to the Fortress. *Strada privata*, said a notice, but I ignored it. There was a track of beaten red earth through the green wheatfield. I could hear larks. The sun had come out. It was beautiful. The track dipped down into the valley. I could not help breathing rather more quickly. Then I saw that all the scrub, except on the hillsides, had been cleared away and the ground bulldozed, so that the quantities of little, deep, jungly rivulets, with creepers like lianas, that I had known before had disappeared now channelled into a single stream running down the centre, the Moletta itself I suppose. The soil had been ploughed to a rich Devon colour and looked wonderfully fertile.

I had expected everything to seem much smaller, but now the centre had been cleared the Fortress had become larger, the distances greater. There was a lot of broom, and elders were in flower. I saw asphodels, poppies, convolvulus. Above all the valley was full of the song of nightingales; the volume of their singing was incredible. The Fortress had turned into one of the loveliest places in the world, and the most peaceful, just as I imagine that Roman Campagna to have been one hundred and fifty years ago.

Those nightingales – I thought I would never want to hear them again. It seemed so odd that the worse things were, the harder they would want to sing. . . . From our ridge at night we could watch the grenades exploding like fiery cactus dahlias round our old area; even more bizarre was the tracer, whipping up and down the valley, looking far more lethal than we had ever realized.

In spite of the bulldozing, I could easily make out where that first platoon area had been. When I got to the spot, however, I couldn't see a single trace of war, not even a dent. I knew exactly where on the slope I had myself laid scores of pencil mines in 1944, and I was ashamed to find that I was still afraid to walk up there, until my companion pointed out the many criss-cross tracks made by sheep and cattle. So I climbed bravely to the top and took an artistic photograph, with a piece of yellow broom in the foreground. It looked so very rural down there, so arcadian. In a way I felt I could even be happy if I had to live in a house in that valley.

The sun was beginning to set. There was only time for a quick visit to Cicada Valley, and I was glad. Now I was indeed struck, very forcefully, by the absurdity, the danger of my old platoon position. The wadi was a mere declivity, and the German machine-guns had been waiting, literally, over the brow. Perhaps it had been lucky for both sides that we hadn't known just how close we were to each other. . . . Those graves had mostly belonged to people of the Queen's and North Staffs. My companion was surprised that it was all so 'domestic'. The German trenches, and ours, he said, were like houses in next-door streets in a suburban village. There was scarcely any room for fighting.

While I was at Cicada Valley I had done another terrible thing. I had sniped a German. In a way I had had to do it out of self-preservation, but now that I look back on the incident I realize I did it to show off in front of the men – and I was very aware afterwards that they had admired me for it. That was another traumatic moment in my military career.

The second-in-command of our company, a very sensitive man, now an architect, was quite amused by my boasting. . . . I had been chiefly shocked, I think, because I had felt no hatred for the man whom I had killed. If I had felt no fury, I certainly had felt no hatred towards any of the 'Krauts' in front of us. In any case most of our immediate opponents were not Germans but Ukrainians, and they certainly – or so we imagined – couldn't have hated *us*.

One's emotions in war, or rather a young man's emotions, can be hopelessly illogical. Less than a week before the sniping of my German, or Ukrainian, I had been somewhat upset by an incident in which I had also, if unwillingly, been involved. Through my field glasses I had observed that, just before dusk and always at exactly the same time every evening, three Krauts would file along a skyline 200 yard away, each carrying a couple of buckets. Obviously they were bringing food to some unit or other.

Everyone at H.Q. became violently excited. That party of food carriers must be wiped out. What fun to make the German (or Ukrainian) unit go hungry for a night. So in due course a concentration of mortar fire was brought down on those three men as they trotted along their skyline, and they were wiped out. The glee at H.Q., and the self-congratulation, nagged at me. Yet two days later I was able, quite calmly, to snipe a machine-gunner combing his hair in the sunlight. . . . Come to think of it, the second-in-command must have been at H.Q. too. It never dawned on me at the time, though admittedly I do not remember if he was among the people who had upset me.

I was not especially anxious to visit the Anzio war cemetery. Nevertheless, having come all that way, and having gone to the trouble of hiring a car, an undefined sort of obligation impelled me there. It was getting ever darker, and Cicada Valley had depressed me. We returned to our Fiat and drove quickly to the end of the Lateral Road, where I saw with some amazement that the Flyover Bridge was still in its war-shattered state, girders sticking out, concrete crumbling, just as I had seen it in Imperial War Museum photographs taken (God help us) nearly a quarter of a century ago. The Italians, having obliterated everything else to do with the Beachhead, had thoughtfully left that one monument, so that an old blimp like myself could turn to his companion and say, 'You see, I was right after all.'

South Koreans, I believe, like going for picnics in American war cemeteries. Well, Anzionians (if one calls them that) would find much to impress them if they decided to take their salami and bel paese sandwiches to their local British war cemetery. For I can truthfully, if reluctantly, say that it is delightful, dignified and serene; the rows of plain, identical Carrara stones wonderfully set off the scarlet rambler roses on the pergolas between the plots. And in among the graves there are pinks, weigela, rosemary. I salute the War Graves people, and the British love of gardening.

I went to look at my friend Monty's grave, the one who had died at the Calypso. Near him were all the others who had died on 23rd May, including Corporal Peter. Everybody, I noticed, had been aged between nineteen and twenty-two. Further away, and breaking the symmetry a little, were two groups of newer graves. The unknown soldiers, whose bodies had been found more recently. In front of these were big stretches of empty lawn, waiting for more bodies – or for another war.

In recent years I have read many books about the strategy of the Beachhead landings, and I have even been goaded to write bitter articles about the generals and politicians who planned it. After all, the men in my platoon had every reason to believe – as I did – that their leaders, those in the very highest positions, were working to some sort of co-ordinated plan, and at least knew what they were doing. In war, at that low level, one just has to imagine that those at the top are supermen, never affected by jealousy, tiredness, fear, illness or impatience. We never thought to question this at the Fortress; nor, I am sure, did the Scots Guards at Carroceto, or the Sherwood Foresters at Campoleone.

I now know from those books that we were all utterly mistaken. 'Operation Shingle' was a mess and a flop. From 22nd January to 23rd May there were 35,000 British and American combat casualties, not counting air and sea losses, and 40,000 non-combat casualties. If it paid off, it was for reasons never envisaged by its perpetrators, reasons like providing lessons on how not to behave during the Second Front in Normandy.

'Political rather than military considerations dominated the decision at Tunis to go ahead with Shingle', says Mark Clark, the 5th Army commander and a character who has always particularly enraged me. He was writing then of Churchill, who had been granted Anzio as a sort of toy after an illness. 'The whole affair has a strong odour of Gallipoli and apparently the same amateur was on the coach's bench,' wrote the disastrous General Lucas, wary, gloomy, pessimistic, in his diary: and he was to be the American general in charge of the landings.

Alexander admits in his autobiography that a month had to pass before he could persuade Clark to get rid of Lucas. He could only do this by reminding Clark that it would be 'very bad' if the Allies were pushed into the sea; it might cost Clark his own command in fact. 'This gentle injunction,' he says mildly, 'impelled action.' Alexander's very calmness was to make him tower at Cassino, but one wonders what would have happened at Anzio if Clark had been faced with a superior of fiercer temperament and closer to his own ilk. And old 'Jumbo' Wilson, sitting at Caserta as Supreme Allied Commander, shouldn't he have briefed Churchill more thoroughly in the first place about how the Americans were emasculating Shingle?

The argument will always continue, to the end of time no doubt, as to whether Lucas should have driven straight on to Rome, or at least to the Alban Hills, after landing without any opposition whatsoever at Anzio and Nettuno. Couldn't he have shown just a little daring, a little bluff instead of digging in a mere six miles' distance from Anzio and waiting for Kesselring to mass his forces for a straightforward, old-fashioned counter-attack? Churchill's 'wildcat', in his characteristically expressive phrase, had indeed turned into a stranded whale, and a wounded, bleeding whale at that. To me Anzio will always be a classic example of British and American wartime incompatibility.

Driving back to Rome in my Fiat, along that very road on which Lucas should have advanced to victory in January, 1944, I started fulminating all over again about generals' mistakes and weaknesses. Then, suddenly, I found myself becoming unaccountably more charitable. It is easy to look for scapegoats, to be wise after the event, especially when the people one is insulting are mostly dead themselves.

I, too, had done stupid, disastrous, dreadful things at Anzio. I had been frightened, exhausted, vain. Lucas, after all, had distinguished himself quite well after Salerno. Even generals are human beings. My return to Anzio had woken me up to that, if to nothing else. I also realized that I was nearly forty-five, an age when men do sometimes become generals. I could never be a general (thank God); if I were I would probably make a far worse hash of things in a situation like Shingle.

Anyhow I had done with Anzio. I'd played my part of warrior returning, and I would never dream of revisiting the Moletta, the Fortress or Cicada Valley, if I could help it. I had had my experience; that was now past.